THE POET AS CITIZEN

LONDON
Cambridge University Press
FETTER LANE

TORONTO
BOMBAY · CALCUTTA · MADRAS
Macmillan

TOKYO
Maruzen Company Ltd

Copyrighted in the United States
of America by
THE MACMILLAN COMPANY

All rights reserved

THE POET AS CITIZEN

AND OTHER PAPERS

BY

SIR ARTHUR QUILLER-COUCH, M.A.

FELLOW OF JESUS COLLEGE
KING EDWARD VII PROFESSOR OF ENGLISH LITERATURE
IN THE UNIVERSITY OF CAMBRIDGE

CAMBRIDGE
AT THE UNIVERSITY PRESS
1934

Catalogued.

PRINTED IN GREAT BRITAIN

CONTENTS

PREFACE vii

THE POET AS CITIZEN

I. ANCIENT AND MODERN NOTIONS . 1
II. THE CULT OF PERSONALITY. . 25
III. TRADITION AND ORTHODOXY . 44

FIRST AID IN CRITICISING

I. ON BEING DEFINITE . . 66
II. A NOTE ON THE *POETICS* . . 86
III. THE HANDICAP OF POETRY . . 104
IV. WORDS AND NATURE . . 121

PATERNITY IN SHAKESPEARE . . 137
TENNYSON IN 1833 . . . 161
WILLIAM BARNES . . . 174
THE EARLIER NOVELS OF THOMAS HARDY 197
TRIBUTE TO IRELAND . . . 218

INDEX 227

PREFACE

OF the following pages all but *Tennyson in 1833* and *Tribute to Ireland* (these reprinted from '*The Times* Literary Supplement' by permission) were given as lectures; hence their colloquial style. *Paternity in Shakespeare* was read before the British Academy as its annual Shakespeare Lecture in 1932. My Cambridge audience endured the rest.

The title 'First Aid in Criticising' advertises four of these as elementary: and so of purpose they were. Few can admire more than I the hard thinking put into their work by some (and notably here in Cambridge) of the new race of 'psychological' critics, as I may call them; or hope more of their earnest sincerity. But the vocabulary of their science is not yet determined; they invent new words and locutions as they press along, and in such haste that *B* may too easily mistake what *A* precisely means by this or that abstract term, even if *A* shall have fixed it to his own mental satisfaction. Further, this concentration on Æsthetic tends more and more of late to distract the attention from the essential in any given work to let curiosity play upon (*a*) the reader, his 'resilience' or 'awareness' or 'sense of immediacy'; which at once transfers concern from the thing itself to So-and-So's *ego* and—there being so many of us in the world and our occasions so various—dissipates study: or (*b*) upon the private life of the author; e.g. of Wordsworth, not upon what he expressly wrote for our advantage in *The Prelude* but upon what someone guesses he set out to conceal.

For these reasons it seemed opportune to remind a

youthful audience of some methods which, though elementary, have been observed by critics admittedly not puerile.

The paper *Tribute to Ireland*, a 'review', hints at a debt of enjoyment and instruction which it must suffice for the while that I acknowledge. Our professional critics take the conventions of their trade with such a depressing solemnity that they dismiss as negligible the beautiful art of gay writing in which our literature has constantly excelled. It were a chastening discipline for reviewers who week by week hail any turgid German novel as a masterpiece, to set them down to a page of *The Irish R.M.* or any of its successors, and invite them to better a sentence, to suggest the slightest improvement on the artistry. And this provokes a wider surmise —What would be the future loss not only to us but to all Europe if an Irish Republic, having its way, were to compel all its authors to sing and write in Gaelic? With Burke, Goldsmith, Sheridan, Blake, Synge, Æ, Yeats in our minds—to omit a score—we may faintly guess our own literature lacking the delicate cadence, the 'sweet wild twist' of the Irish idiom. But that Europe at large and at this time of day is likely (on any translated evidence at least) to be charmed by much in a separatist language imposed by a 'government' seems to me a delusion and a dream. Great literatures are not grown in that way.

ARTHUR QUILLER-COUCH

Jesus College, Cambridge
  Trafalgar Day, 1934

THE POET AS CITIZEN. I

ANCIENT & MODERN NOTIONS

I

I PROPOSE, Gentlemen, to consider with you the right place of Poetry in a well-ordered Commonwealth, and the right value of the Poet as a citizen. Ideally perhaps these two enquiries should be one: but historically they are neither identical, nor coincident, nor even correspondent in their ups and downs. I need not remind you for example, that in Athens, at its very acme of attainment in the Arts and eminently in serving that sisterhood of the poetic Muse for whom nine several statues claimed worship, already the prince of political philosophers was starting a doubt if these poets as purveyors of lies upon lies should not be escorted out of a decently organised State and affectionately dismissed over its frontier into some such easy-going receptacle as Corinth, where the profiteers were. Nor need you be reminded of instances—they will occur to you by the score—of Villon, greatest poet of his time, picking purses and gnawing crusts under the gallows; of Marlowe, Peele, Greene—the whole melancholy calendar of our own poetical Alsatias; of Stepney, Grub Street, Bridewell, Bedlam, Sponging house, Mad house, Poor house—

Toil, envy, want, the patron and the gaol,

THE POET AS CITIZEN

with the too-late recognition and repentance—

> See nations, slowly wise and meanly just,
> To buried merit raise the tardy bust.

The iniquity of it is accepted, proverbial, and goes back even to legend, to Homer—

> Seven wealthy towns contend for Homer dead
> Through which the living Homer begged his bread[1]

—an epigram in all likelihood quite untrue to fact but strictly true to human experience down to this day.

II

Now in accounting for this treatment of the Poet by his fellow-citizens let me start by ruling out almost all that the philosophers have said in his disparagement: and this for two reasons; the first being that what they say is untrue; the second that, whether true or not, it has never in practice mattered. I suppose that never in history has a Poet starved because a Philosopher said he should. That the author of *Venice Preserved* in his ravening hunger choked himself with a loaf charitably bestowed by a passer-by cannot be laid at Plato's door or imputed against any high-browed frequenter of the low-browed roof of Socrates. We need not consent with Goldsmith's Chinaman, Lien Chi Altangi, Citizen of the World—'You see, my friend, there is nothing so ridiculous that it has not at some time been said by some

---

[1] Attributed to Thomas Seward (1708–90), but anyhow an improved theft from Thomas Heywood's (d. 1650?):

> Seven cities warred for Homer being dead
> Who living had no roof to shield his head.

philosopher'. It is enough that over the inveterate and one-sided quarrel between Philosophy and Poetry—one-sided because the philosophers do all the invective and explanation, while the poets drop a stray compliment to assure them, for example, that they are not harsh and crabbed, as dull fools suppose, and go on writing poetry—the world in general no more takes an active concern than will a discreet man in a squabble between husband and wife. The world, in fact—or that part of it to which Poetry is or has ever been addressed—is, whether consciously or not, the ultimate judge and a sane critic wiser than any philosopher: as Bagehot insisted, quoting a certain 'great man of the world' whom he omits to name. 'There is someone wiser than Voltaire and wiser than Napoleon, *c'est tout le monde*.' 'Popular judgment on popular matters (Bagehot adds) is crude and vague', but it is astonishingly right.

'All very well,' you will say; 'but if Poetry be not a popular matter, as we hold it should be, the saying misses in application. And if the world's judgment be right, why not right *in time*? Why should so many whose monuments we scan with reverence have asked for bread in life and been given posthumously a Stone?'

Is there a reason for it save as Dr Johnson might have put it, 'No, Sir; none save stark insensibility!'?

III

In seeking, then, the answer to that question—which, blunt though it sound, really involves the relation of the arts, and of Poetry in especial, to national life (or shall I say to life in a community of civilised men)—we shall not go to-day to the philosophers, or at any rate shall not begin by consulting them. We need not accuse them of prejudice in any bad sense: for the question touches, at least, on ethics, which is their province; may easily be taken prisoner, thrust into a dungeon and strangled by stern morality: and it has been well said that in most questions of morality the reasons by which men arrive at their conclusions are of little importance; what is of importance is the fact that they reach certain results and rest in them. 'Men ride their arguments as children their horses. They put their legs over a stick, run far afield, and make believe that the stick has carried them.' So men take Plato's conclusion that poets should be banished from a model Republic and take it seriously because it is Plato's, without looking under the skirts of the hobby on which Plato arrived at this: without examining, for instance, his demonstration that art is false because the thing it copies is itself a copy of the divine Idea, and bad because it aims at pleasure which is no less unknown to the Gods than pain. And with Plato this same author that I have been quoting (E. S. Dallas) in that most undeservedly neglected book *The Gay Science* (*Le Gai Saber*) instances Tertullian as denouncing tragedians because by wearing buskins they gave the lie to Christ, who said that no man could add a cubit to his stature, and even Bacon who, thinking usury wicked, argues it wicked because it runs on Sundays!

Asking the philosophers then to stand back a while, let us cite any cultivated man of the world who after all

ANCIENT AND MODERN NOTIONS

is the real defendant on this charge of neglect. And let us put it thus to him—

You are a man on whose education your parents spent a considerable sum, sending you first to a Public School and afterwards to an English University?
Answer: Yes, to Cambridge.
Question: Capital! And what did you read there?
Answer: For the Classical Tripos: and afterwards I should have read for the English Tripos: but it scarcely existed in my time. 'My time' I should explain is a current phrase for anyone's period of residence. It does not necessarily mark an epoch.
Question: Modestly spoken: and after that?
Answer: I secured, by competition, a post in H.M. Civil Service from which I shall shortly retire on a moderate pension.
Question: And did you at Cambridge—traditional nurse of poets—imbibe a taste for Poetry?
Answer: A passion, rather. Keats... Wordsworth.... Poetry has been my companion through life—my constant resource.
Question: Your companion? Resource—from what? Are you married?
Answer: Yes: but, you see, my wife is a practical woman, and—
Question: I understand. Those are often said to make the happiest union. Children?
Answer: One son: seventeen: has matriculated at London University, with honours in English.
Question: And he inherits your passion for Poetry?

Answer: Well, I suppose so. He's inclined to be shy with his father and I hope it's not altogether my fault. But he has always the run of my library—a pretty representative one I can tell you. I keep myself abreast of the moderns even. But of course...Didn't I say he had taken honours in English?

...and so on....The man is shy about it. I suggest there is something in Poetry which makes men and women, after the age of youthful eager friendships, hide away the appeal of Poetry—and especially the emotional appeal as a whisper in their own bosoms.

IV

But let us fly at higher game, and interrogate (say) some distinguished Professor of History, putting our first question thus—

(1) The story of Man on this planet is very old and overspread with layer upon layer of dead dynasties, dead civilisations, dead religions. How much should we know of these were it not for the beautiful things—statue and cup, armour, jewel, song—the various artists designed for men's delight—yes, delight in their day? 'It is in art' (here I quote Dallas again) 'that the history of the world is enshrined—almost in art alone that the far past survives.' And he goes on 'Men's works of labour die: their works of pleasure live'. This, as we shall see, will have to be qualified, yet only by a little. In the main it holds good, and of Poetry in particular: even of Poetry as against Religion. The late Sir William Ridgeway, that strong teacher, once startled his class

ANCIENT AND MODERN NOTIONS

here by a casual assertion—'Religions pass, theogonies have their day and fashion, but the Muse abides'—or words to that effect. He was not meaning the religious instinct, but its forms of expression: whereas the forms, the actual words in which men have clothed their poetic instinct, remain as fresh and lively to-day as the instinct itself—as, for example, the *Bacchae* remains a thing of beauty to-day, however we may disapprove of the misbehaviour on Cithaeron.

And as with religions, so more evidently with dynasties. What history knows of Egypt it has learnt mainly from the works of art found in royal tombs under the sand, pathetically laid there, thousands of years ago, to delight dead rulers in another world. The rulers themselves—Thothmes, Rameses, Ptolemy, Shepherd King and Priest King—are a tale decipherable only through these flatteries of the artist:

> I will hew thee a tomb!
> "All the kings of the nations lie in glory";
> Cased in cedar and shut in a sacred gloom;
> Swathed in linen, and precious unguents old;
> Painted in cinnabar, and rich with gold.
>
> Silent they rest, in solemn salvatory,
> Sealed from the moth and the owl and the flitter-mouse—
> Each with his name on his brow
> "All the kings of the nations lie in glory,
> Every one in his own house":

—the inhabitants of these houses are as dust on the sand around and above:

> Here are sands, ignoble things,
> Dropt from the ruin'd sides of kings.

To be sure as we come nearer to our own day our knowledge of the past grows less and less dependent on these relics of the Artist and the Poet, simply because we emerge into *historic* times; with events documented in chronicles, public records, private letters; till at length we reach that grand preservative, the Printing Press. Also the relics themselves multiply, because we come into our own recent civilisation, and the teeth of moth and rust, weather and housemaids, have had less time to eat into the mass. Also, again, we are near enough to the events themselves to have our own lives sensibly qualified by them, and felt as so qualified. And this again is a point. We may stand on the Cape of Trafalgar and tell ourselves in an expansive moment that the swell in the offing rolls as heedlessly over that scene as into the gulfs of Lepanto or of Salamis. But actually we are not what we should have been, either in substance or in spirit, in circumstance or in faith, if Themistocles, if Don John of Austria had not swooped there, and there, and Nelson here. We feel what the wave cannot obliterate—the deed: as, more faintly perhaps, we feel that we are different because of it.

Of prehistoric times, then, Horace states but the plain truth—'Many strong men lived before Agamemnon, but all these are packed away into long night, unwept, unknown, lacking a divine bard'. But come to historic times, even to times brilliantly historic, and suppose for a moment the zenith of Athens herself. Remove from your minds—leaving behind her polity, her wars, her philosophers, geometers, astronomers, her sophists even: remove from your minds all relics of its

ANCIENT AND MODERN NOTIONS

drama with what that drama tells us of Athens. Wipe the Parthenon itself off the hill, and then try to conceive how much less the name of Athens would mean to our imagination, to our understanding, to-day. Rome spared it in honour because these monuments still stood, in Rome's day, visible in stone and scarcely impaired, its masterpieces of poetry still extant and whole, to be read and copied by a less imaginative but prudently acquisitive race. But before this the enquiring Alexander had lowered his lance to the Muse in homage.

> Lift not thy spear against the Muse's bower.
> The great Emathian conqueror bid spare
> The house of Pindarus, when temple and tower
> Went to the ground: and the repeated air
> Of sad Electra's poet had the power
> To save the Athenian walls from ruin bare.

From Athens let us descend, from a purpose presently to be used, upon the island of Lesbos. What do we know, save from a passage or two in Herodotus, Diodorus, and others about the considerable island of Lesbos and its ultimate and in its day very considerable capital—Mytilene? We may hazily remember that it was inhabited by the Aeolian Greeks, that its valleys were fertile in corn, that its hills grew on their lower slopes a once famous, now forgotten, wine. To-day the world remembers Lesbos not as once the throne of Makar and his family, but as the birthplace of four makers of song—Arion, inventor of the dithyramb and the earlier lyrists, Terpander, Alcaeus, Sappho—above all Sappho.

V

(2) This brings me to my second point. A lyric of Sappho was recovered the other day from an Egyptian dust-heap. But—if you think of it—people do not—did not, even when papyrus was expensive—copy down things on the back of washing bills and the like (of receipted ones at any rate) unless to be put aside for remembrance. So next I ask you to consider the astonishing proportion held by works of fine art (including great poetry) in the *detritus* left to us by past ages. It is so high, compared with the proportion between gold and dross familiar to us in our own daily observation, that it upsets all rules of rarity and beats the connoisseur at his own game.

We may find reasons, of course and easily, which go some way to account for it. Pious men, for instance, who give commissions for votive offerings desire them to be of costly and durable material. On such material the best artist is glad to work: it taxes his skill, attests his present eminence, and promises that his fame will survive him. Rich plate, delicate laces and embroideries, even brittle glasses of curious workmanship, are kept as heirlooms and sometimes protected by legend. Good housewives do not allow their best porcelain to be slammed down on the too 'free' breakfast table. But let me fetch an example and a true parable from my own modest cupboard.

Some ninety years ago a middle-aged naturalist was disturbed in his writing by wife and maid: 'There was a man at the door hawking this wonderful invention'.

ANCIENT AND MODERN NOTIONS

'Ah yes,' said the naturalist, taking it—a packet of very small sticks—'Lucifer matches—I have heard of them. Go out, my dear, and buy all he has to sell': and—to the maid, 'You Bessie, go to the kitchen, fetch your tinderbox off the chimney shelf and bring it here, exactly as it is, that I may lock it away'. 'But', said his wife, 'why lock away that old thing costing twopence, when there's a fine brass one at your elbow, another upstairs and my grandmother's handsome copper one in the diningroom?' 'Why, because in less than six months the tide below us will have washed away all the tin tinder-boxes in this town, whereas in ten years' time your fine ones will be left so common as to be worth no man's collecting.' That is how I come to possess a rusty tinder-box, with flint, steel, sulphur-tipped sticks, tinder and some ashes of paper inside, all just as the maid fetched it that morning. I suppose it to be worth considerably more than twopence, while not valuing that sort of thing myself.

Anyhow it has served a purpose by providing me with just that exception which proves the rule—the rule that men, having done with them, throw away the tools and utensils of work-a-day life. I dare say that handsome old tinder-boxes, if not already, will soon be, the collector's quarry; but they will never be so rare as my twopenny tin one abides because a queer mind looked around a generalisation and presented it from the back as a paradox.

It may take you a moment's thinking to fit this illustration in with the wonderful survival of great poetry of the Greek and Latin Classics, as we call them, across centuries of Moslem and Turk, religious hatred, blind barbarism, zeal of Christian Fathers, mere neglect by the chance inheritors of manuscripts; by monks taught to hold poetry sinful, more pardonably by great nobles of whom the most had the sufficient excuse of never having learnt to read. We may deplore the extent of the loss: still the proportionate amount of the survival and the quality of it remain miraculous. Or you may argue that, literature being memorable speech transmitted to record, the best has survived because it was most memorable: and yet the marvel remains. It has been computed that no less than 700,000 rolls of manuscript perished in successive burnings of the great libraries of Alexandria. What are the 50 or more lost plays of Euripides in comparison with all that mass, which sufficed to heat the public baths for six months? As Gibbon remarks of the catastrophe, 'When I seriously compute the lapse of ages, the waste of ignorance and the calamities of war, our treasures, rather than our losses, are the objects of my surprise'.

What intelligence then, or what Providence, has sifted out (with heavy losses) our remarkable inheritance of poetry? Certainly, as we have seen, the philosophers did not: and as certainly not the official Church, which for centuries condemned Poetry on the ground that it gave pleasure: while the critics up to this happy age, even when they agree in discovering six or eight masterpieces weekly, accuse one another of being more often wrong than right.

VI

But this brings us back again to the original question: and before attempting an answer, let us add one or two further charges to the Poets' complaint.

(3) So—let us say, thirdly, they can assert as a plain fact that Poetry has engaged upon its business the strongest intellects in our known history, and that not as a πάρεργον or relaxation, but as a part at least of their most serious business in life. Who can deny this sheer power to Aeschylus, to Pindar, to Lucretius, to Dante, to Leonardo da Vinci, to Michelangelo, to Carducci, to Racine, to Hugo, to Goethe: to our own tremendous Milton, manly Dryden, serious Wordsworth, equally serious Shelley? How came Poetry to engage, to captivate the massive practical intellect of Samuel Johnson? Surely that last single question suffices to carry the answer.

VII

The poets themselves, of course, have no doubt whatever concerning the value, present and permanent, of their wares; and we must listen to them with due reverence, albeit with such reasonable caution as we should use in ordinary life towards persons who write their own testimonials; as again we must be careful not to confuse their claims for Poetry with their claims for themselves. Ben Jonson, for instance, very great man as he was, thought appreciably more of himself than his contemporaries did, and possibly just a trifle more than any later age is ever quite likely to do. Of another very great man—Wordsworth—we may not perhaps say that his self-esteem was exorbitant, taken in itself: taken in comparison with his estimate of other poets it suggests some doubt. You remember his assuring Charles Lamb that 'he could have written *Paradise Lost* if he'd had the mind to', with Lamb's retort; and (if Hazlitt can be trusted) his pronouncement on Burns—'Mr Wordsworth hints that, with different personal habits and greater strength of mind, Burns would have written differently, and almost as well as *he* does'. While Keats lived, Shelley did not think much of him; and Matthew Arnold in turn was curiously insensitive to Shelley.

But take these names I have quoted, and you will find them all at one in endorsing the proud claim of Poetry, of their art, upon mankind. Ben Jonson puts it with characteristic arrogance—'Every beggarly Corporation affords a Mayor or two Bailiffs yearly, but *Solus rex aut poeta non quotannis nascitur*—You don't get a king or a poet every 9th of November'.

Wordsworth claims for the Poet that he is 'the rock and defender of human nature': and again 'Aristotle, I have been told'—but he must have been told inaccurately—'hath said that poetry is the most philosophic of all writings'. '*It is so*', he adds magisterially. Then comes an outburst of eloquence.—'In spite of difference of soil and climate, of language and manners, of laws and customs; in spite of things silently gone out of mind and things violently destroyed, the Poet binds together the vast empire of human society as it is spread over the whole earth and over all time.' One can scarcely exaggerate upon *that*. And so, to save time, I omit equal or like claims by the others I have mentioned—

ANCIENT AND MODERN NOTIONS

Keats, Shelley, Arnold. And you have to allow that even when they boast it of *themselves*, to outlast dynasties, a good number of these poets prophesied *truly*, even of their lighter verse. Horace claimed that in his alcaics and sapphics he had carved out a monument more durable than brass: *and it is*. Or hear Landor—

> Past ruin'd Ilion Helen lives;
> Alcestis rises from the shades.
> Verse calls them forth; 'tis verse that gives
> Immortal youth to mortal maids.

Or descend to Herrick, reluctant swain of rusticity—

> Trust to good verses then;
> They only will aspire
> When pyramids as men
> Are lost i' th' funeral fire.
>
> And when all bodies meet
> In Lethe to be drown'd,
> Then only numbers sweet
> With endless life are crown'd.

Sublime confidence! yet to this day justified. For Julia's petticoat and silken bracelets have outlived three centuries or so of fashions, and

> The Elves also
> Whose little eyes glow

still attend and sparkle on the essential Julia, on whatever nocturnal errand stealing.

VIII

Yet here again we have to make several discounts.

To begin with, we have been considering good poets, real poets, leaving mediocre ones and bad ones out of the reckoning. And, as Horace says of the former even—

> mediocribus esse poetis
> Non homines, non di, non concessere columnae
> But gods, and men, and publishers agree
> To place their ban on middling poetry

and often on bad, I am told. Now the trouble here with the middling and bad poets is in the first place, of course, that there are so many of them; and secondly (I speak of a long experience) that they are more touchy and self-assertive than their betters. Horace knew them and rather cruelly insisted on some physical characteristics, more irrelevant than they should be—

> long nails and untrimmed hair;
> Much in brown studies, in the bath-room rare.

We have not to do with these, although in actual life they are a considerable nuisance, and actually, with their airs and epicene voices, help the prejudice against which we would fight. We talk of better poets.

IX

Even so we find that the esteem of Poetry as a racial or national possession, and the consequent esteem of the Poet as a citizen, have varied violently from one age to another, and even in the same community. To the whole Hellenic world, scattered though the tradition was over an age of enquiry, 'Homer' stood for Holy Writ. We find him quoted with awe, as old-fashioned Protestants quoted the Bible, holding it verbally inspired: and this throughout, often to our surprise, when Homer happens (as he not infrequently does) to be saying nothing in particular. But for the Greeks—his antiquity aiding—the *Iliad* and *Odyssey* held their racial religion, if in solution. You all know how Aeschylus crystallised that religion, or part of it, and was venerated by Athens therefore. But let me take, for one illustration out of many, the less known story of Tyrtaeus. It goes that in the seventh century B.C., in the course of their second war against their fellow Dorians of Messene, the Spartans were advised by an Oracle to choose a leader from Attica. They therefore applied to the Athenians: and the Athenians, unwilling to help their rivals in conquering the whole Peloponnese, purposely sent them one Tyrtaeus, a lame schoolmaster of low birth. But Tyrtaeus happened to be a poet; whose songs so animated the Spartans that they broke Messene, that great stronghold, and conquered. 'A legend', you say? Yes, if you will, as much a legend as that of Amphion who drew stones together with his singing—*movit lapides canendo*—and so built a city even as Tyrtaeus destroyed one. Yes, but a legend, however exaggerated upon fact, *is its own fact*, witnessing belief. Welshmen in our day who chant *Land of Our Fathers* at a football match before a cup-tie; while the English, on an evocation hard to explain, retort *Abide with me*! Strange the challenge, stranger the retort! Yet, it may be, the impulse has degenerated from that nobler one which commanded Pindar's tremendous strains to celebrate a patron's victory in a chariot-race or a town's exultation over some boy-boxer's success. Suppose to yourselves the laureate of our day commanded to hymn next year's Derby winner: to work in not only the horse's but its noble owner's noble genealogies, with laudifications of Newmarket, Manton, Epsom, Kingsclere as it might be, to be sung on Derby night by backers and bookmakers in strophe and anti-strophe. Yet that was what Pindar disdained not.

Or consider Landor's beautiful lines put in the mouth of Corinna, a lady who had taught Pindar and, once at least, won the crown from him in her maturity.

CORINNA, FROM ATHENS TO TANAGRA
[*her native town*]

>   Tanagra! think not I forget
>   Thy beautifully-storey'd streets....
>   I promise to bring back with me
>   What thou with transport wilt receive
>   The only proper gift for thee,
>   Of which no mortal shall bereave
>   In later times thy mouldering walls
>   Until the last old turret falls;
>   A crown, a crown from Athens won,
>   A crown no god can wear, beside Latona's son!
>   There may be cities that refuse
>   To their own child the honours due,
>   And look ungently on the Muse;
>   But ever shall those cities rue
>   The dry, unyielding, niggard breast,
>   Offering no nourishment, no rest
>   To that young head which soon shall rise
>   Disdainfully, in might and glory, to the skies.

Mark, further, that even when Socratic questioning, followed up by Plato, is well on its way to disintegrate the high tradition, and Euripides is posing religion with casuistry in his handling of ancient themes, *still* the very seriousness of the attack confesses the Poet's importance. He is there, and has been. If an enemy, or if a somebody irreconcilable with the philosopher's idea of a perfect citizen, he is anyhow a *civic* nuisance, and one so troublesome to our theory that he must be got rid of, though it cost the drastic process of dismissing him into exile.

And here I may pause to remind you that Plato, who could confirm his theory to advise this, invariably, when logical reasoning leads him to the edge of mystery into which he sees darkly but which he cannot by reason expound, dives out of logic, dives into poetry and escapes in the beautiful clouds of a myth. Still, in Athens men were writing poetry and were writing it *for the present—their present*. It was only when these poets were dead or had ceased to write, that poetry became lifeless, listless, a study for Alexandria, for Grammarians, a body to dissect.

X

So it happened (I think) with Hebrew Literature when absorbed and re-issued to the Gentiles as a well-spring of Christian faith. You have only to flutter the pages of our Revised Version—which as a sort of first-aid, by arrangement of type, helps you rather half-heartedly to distinguish verse from prose—to discover how great a proportion of the Old Testament is poetry, and intentional poetry: and next on a little examination, to discover that—bating Job, a few Psalms, the Song of Songs, Ecclesiastes—all this poetry is racial, or tribal. 'Israel', 'Sion', 'My people', 'The stars in their courses fought against Sisera', 'General of Canaan', 'The river Kishon swept them away': that ancient river the river Kishon (which by the by had watered the Canaanites long before Israel crossed it). 'So let thine (that is, our) enemies perish, O Lord!' Or 'Comfort ye, comfort ye, my people, saith your God. Speak ye comfortably to Jerusalem, say unto her that her warfare is accomplished'. Or 'Arise, shine; for thy light is come... and nations shall come to thy light, and kings to the brightness of thy rising'. So Deborah curses the inhabitants of Meroz because they came not to the help of the Lord, just as the Achaeans saw Amyclae a vast wilderness for ever, damned by a moment's silence, when its townsmen could have spoken a pan-Hellenic word, and did not.

The Hellenes—remind yourselves—were, equally with the Jews, an exclusive race, fissiparous among themselves, jealous, critical of one another as (shall we say?) any cluster of Victorian aunts and mothers: speaking no language but their own, scornful of barbarians or Gentiles. I think we should bear this in mind even while we marvel at what Athens achieved. By her own arts she achieved her own perfection, a lesson to all, and rested on that. But the doom of any perfection in this restless life of man is that it must incite to experiment, to attempt to improve upon the best, else it is static, inert, dead.

That, however, has been a brief digression. To revert in a few words to Israel. Its poets were consciously, intensively racial: and Israel certainly did not stone the prophets because they wrote bad verse, or because they wrote good verse, but because what they wrote was politically true and, to the unwise contemporary mob of Israel, politically exasperating.

XI

Christianity follows: and one must sadly admit that to the Muse Christianity, as interpreted by the early Fathers and later by an official Church, spelt ruin for centuries. I have no time here, nor is it necessary, to do more than state the simple historical fact that from the first the Fathers found anathema in pagan poetry and discouraged the very idea of it; or that in the catastrophe of Rome's fall, the clergy (poetry's professional enemies) were left, in Europe proper, almost the only people who possessed any learning or any desire for learning: or again, that, by consequence, through what our fathers reasonably called the Dark Ages, in Pope's summary:

> The Monks finish'd what the Goths began.

Still less need one expatiate upon the text that 'religion is not always a good thing: it may be a very bad thing'. Let us, remembering Aristotle's definition of the Tragic Hero as a man who, virtuous on the whole, comes to grief through some aberration, look charitably for the causes of this most fatal aberration. There were, as it seems to me, two main causes not wholly separable.

The first was, so to speak, a 'Tale of Two Cities': the attractive withdrawal, conversion ('seduction' would be the right word literally, but that has taken on some invidious sub-intentions, and so we will avoid it)

—withdrawal then, of man's concern with his immediate duties to the city of his habitation in this life, by promise of a better citizenship in a New Jerusalem beyond his ken. Death is the gate to that City, and accepted faith the key to its beatitudes. However true that promise may be; however comforting to millions of poor souls desolate, oppressed, or misjudged as they are or deem they are in this world, the expectancy of deserved redress in another; it belittles the importance of man's civic responsibility here in a way that no Athenian, no Roman, would have understood. It leads inevitably to hermitages, caves, nunneries, and to the repute of their inhabitants as holy because segregated from their fellows, passionately intent on preparing their own souls for a deferred celestial inheritance. Thus we get the sweet sisterly service of Poetry to Theology, when not actively trodden on, at best treated as servile: an ignominy which no tyranny, no religion even, can ever impose permanently on the Muse.

Secondly, the poetry of Greece and Rome had dealt with their gods as hail-fellows, more or less; even while deathless or careless: familiar beings, friendly, understandable; mostly understandable if, catching them in some legendary lapse of continence, we could insert a Zeus or Apollo into the topmost line of our pedigree. You can easily see how hard it was for Poetry, switched out of this friendly and almost domestic play with its deities, to transfer its affection, adoration—let be its technique upon a local background, whether of the groves by Ilissus or the pleached hedgeways of a Mantuan farm—to One Deity, incomprehensible, invisible,

ANCIENT AND MODERN NOTIONS

aloof, above frailty, above argument, in the pure Arctic of His own strict law.

I say only here that these enormous shiftings of man's concern—

(1) from concern for his city into concern for his own soul,
(2) from his cheerful liberty of enquiry to limits laid down by one invisible dictatorship, and interpreted by a close professoriate,

—have in fact and through ages worked to man's detriment, through misunderstanding. To Theology, Mother of the Sciences, Poetry should be as her wisest, eldest, and yet ever loveliest youngest daughter, the first of her handmaidens, enjoying the first-born's share of her love. To return to Corinna's appeal with a wider application—

> O let thy children lean aslant
>   Against the tender Mother's knee,
> And gaze into her face, and want
>   To know what magic there can be
> In words that urge some eyes to dance,
>   While others in a holy trance
> Look up to heaven: be such my praise!
> Why linger? I must haste, or lose the Delphic bays.

Rejecting Poetry, how coarse and cheap is the kind of appeal nowadays offered in congregational worship?

> Oh, for the pearly gates of Heaven,
>   Oh, for the Golden floor!

But surely, surely, Oh for anything more poetical!

That sort of stuff may satisfy, but it does not cure; may ease like an opiate, but cannot heal.

> When half-gods go
> The Gods arrive.

I hope, Gentlemen, to examine with you, next time, this opposition of the Poet as an individual and as a citizen; reconciling them if we can; anyhow convinced that it is worth trying in these perilous days.

THE POET AS CITIZEN. II

THE CULT OF PERSONALITY

I

A YEAR or two ago, as a new set of pupils started with me upon Aristotle's *Poetics*, we halted as usual on the threshold, at the second paragraph: to ask what Aristotle meant by saying that 'the Arts, including even Music, were, in general, forms of Mimesis'—a word usually translated as *Imitation*: and, as on former occasions, after pointing out how hard it is to translate any foreign word—especially if it belong to a bygone age, and yet more especially if it be an abstract term—and keep its precise meaning, I asked for a vote on the nearest English word to fit Mimesis. For plainly mere 'Imitation' will not go far beyond the monkey-instinct. It may in a miserable sense be applied to the plastic arts—painting, sculpture—but it certainly cannot cover anything, high or low—Epic, Tragedy, Lyric, Satire even—that civilised men discern and reckon as Poetry. Even less can it cover Music, or any Music beyond a Toy or Barn-yard Symphony. Well, in former days, some bright voice would suggest 'Representation': another, after a pause, 'Expression'. There might follow 'Interpretation'— an answer which we will lay aside to be considered. But up to the evening of which I speak 'Representation' always carried the vote by a large majority. That evening 'Expression' won. This term reversed the voting, and Socratic enquiry revealed that by 'Expression' every voter meant—not the elementary yet most difficult discipline of putting one's meaning into words—but the unfolding, primarily, of one's own inward self. I could not discover that maturity or experience counted much in the process. What counted was a free emanation of the natal spark and intensive culture of whatever fed it.

II

It follows of course that on any such theory of Poetry, Expression hoists the individual into the saddle and gives him the whip. To put it in another way, its method is to start by turning the eye inwards and proceed to divulge what it finds there, for the good of man. Representation, by contrast, starts by looking outward on the multifarious phenomena of life and life's processes, to find, if it can, a Universal truth or type in these; to refer this back to the poet's alembic, and to re-issue it in some definite exemplary form—a parable, a story, a drama, a systematised poem, an ode; a presented character (such as Hamlet, Antigone, Falstaff, Don Quixote, Tartuffe, My Uncle Toby) or even some line or two that casket, it may be, a daily commonplace. What, for example, is more usual, however emotionally vivid and varied to us, than a sunrise, than the fall of the year, or Death itself? Yet when Milton has written—

THE CULT OF PERSONALITY 27

> Together both, ere the high lawns appear'd
> Under the opening eyelids of the morn,
> We drove a-field—

he has given us a new sunrise, to last us for life: as Shakespeare a new Autumn in

> Bare ruined choirs where late the sweet birds sang.

Or when a lesser poet, Vaughan, apostrophises—

> Dear, beauteous Death! the jewel of the Just,
> Shining nowhere but in the dark—

he fixes, so to speak, a *nuance* in the idea of Death which no doubt has floated in the thought of millions since the beginning of the world, and particularly tantalised the metaphysical poets of his time—Donne, Herbert, Shirley too and others: and mints it anew in a phrase. I have purposely chosen lines familiar to you all and purposely invited the objection. 'Yes, but if you are after a definition, these very lines confute you: the very arrest for us depending on their felicity of *expression*.' 'To be sure', I answer; 'but I was not attempting, or seeking to attempt a definition.' To me definitions, in life, and more particularly in literature, are the devil in a world hag-ridden just now by scientists, and as little applicable to the understanding of life *or* letters, as a book of *Rules of Etiquette* to the unconsciously acquired habits of good-breeding. Any gentle mind surely feels, knows, that no truth in this life can ever be confined separately within a verbal formula: that in the end truth in life, or what truth we can reach, is not for a Calvin, and as little for a Hobbes: that, as Renan put it, 'La Vérité consiste dans les nuances'.

III

But one may avoid definitions and yet indicate a plain difference. While undoubtedly the *impression* of those familiar lines I have quoted takes its mark from the poet himself, after he has passed it through the alembic (as I have called it) of his genius, there may yet be a very sensible difference, a difference in *process*. In not one of the instances just quoted has the poet *started from himself*: he has taken a commonplace easy to anyone, referred it home, passed it through the refining self and re-issued it as ours.

To press this point, let me take another quotation, as fine as familiar, reverting again to that commonest yet daily and locally most various among the world's phenomena—sunrise. As this planet sweeps eastering out of shadow, there is not a moment but daylight is kept busy overtaking its hill. But when Romeo, tearing himself from marriage-bed with Juliet, warns—

> Night's candles are burnt out, and jocund day
> Stands tiptoe on the misty mountain tops;
> I must be gone and live, or stay and die.

—a commoner wit than Shakespeare's—Byron let us say—would have expressed itself differently, more egotistically, sensually. The kind of poet that Byron was, being self-centred, would have summoned an earthquake to attend the dismissal of a short amour, or the snows of High Alp for a cold compress on the wound. The one subjective word in Romeo's cry of torture is 'jocund'—'jocund day'. And, let you tell yourselves, how invariably an introspective poet will reduce the

THE CULT OF PERSONALITY

aspects of nature to subserve his mood: how a lake will be gloomy or melancholy or peaceful, a cliff formidable, a thrush's note 'evocative'. In that moment of parting a smaller wit than Shakespeare's would (I suggest) have made daybreak conform to a common lover's mood and made it 'envious' or disagreeable in some other way. Shakespeare by a noble twist makes the morning bright, careless, universal over the world, however heart-broken this particular pair of lovers.

IV

No: I am seeking with you, Gentlemen, no academic definition: rather indicating, roughly, a difference between the Poet as self-centred, and the Poet as he might be, in use and esteem, to the State.

In the last century Tennyson hardly announced that

The individual withers, and the world is more and more.

—to which a philosopher promptly responded 'I am not sure whether the essence of that thought might not have been expressed in the very opposite terms'. Whichever view was the truer then, I think you will agree with me that, just now, the individual, in the general distress of Europe following war, has the bit between his teeth. In nation after nation there is revolt against Government by reasoned consent and clamour for a dictator, a superman: in education, a theory among many that every child should be left to follow his own bent without restraint. [Have you ever, by the way, encountered any young specimens of that training? The theorists might remind themselves that the Latin has two verbs, *educere* and *educare*, and that 'education' derives from the second of these.] But, to speak more seriously, and to cast more widely—Fifteen years ago men's thoughts turned in revolt from the weariness and beastliness of war towards international consent, towards practice in preventing any renewal of 1914–18. To-day I am convinced that the vast majority of men and women desire that prevention, millions upon millions passionately. The tide was not taken on the flood. To-day, through hesitancy, inertia—actively drained, too, by men who trade in other men's death for private profit—that tide has sensibly ebbed, withdrawn into narrow, separate, nationalist channels: and whoso says 'nationalist' says 'separatist' and is nigher to saying 'individualist' than he chooses to think.

V

But take current literature; and consider, as symptomatic, the vogue just now of biography. It is not a new vogue in the handling of history, although of late it has increased and invaded enormously. Even some sixty-odd years ago—about the date, that is, when I was starting to turn 'Balbus is building a wall' into Latin or something like it, Dallas (the writer whom I recommended to you the other day) had remarked upon this.

It cannot [he says] have escaped the notice of the most cursory observer that of late years history has been growing more and more biographical in its tendency. In the picturesque pages of Macaulay, as in that darker scroll on which Carlyle writes his terrible *Mene mene tekel upharsin*—two extremely opposite types of history—it is impossible not to remark how frequently the

THE CULT OF PERSONALITY

narrative is centred in cabinet pictures of personal traits, illustrative manners and accidental customs. On the other hand, we have learned to magnify so much the importance of individuals that there is scarcely a memoir published nowadays in which the subject is not regarded as of national interest.

—that in 1866, when Carlyle was preaching hero-worship, the strong man, belauding Cromwell alike with Frederick of Prussia. Bethink you how this invasion of biography upon history has been advanced by imitators of Lytton Strachey, to dethrone heroes; by imitators of M. Maurois to account for great men, not objectively, by ascertained fact, but by producing out of their own inner consciousness a picture of some great man after their own image: or again how the publishers crowd their lists with memoirs, reminiscences, diaries, So-and-So's-and-their-Circles, letters of people all but insignificant in their impact upon human affairs: and you will realise how this interpretation of events through A's private interpretation of B's private motives has been growing in fashion.

Now I admire Lytton Strachey's technique as anyone must who has a sense of good writing, and (what is more) I detect a man sincerely kind beneath or between the lines of his most corrosive writing. But his way is dangerous for imitators. I cull this example from a posthumous collection of his writings, recently published, *this* of the 'age of Queen Victoria'—in its very title, loose—

It was an age of self-complacency [What? Newman or Clough, I interject, as examples of *that*!] and self-contradiction. Even its atheists were religious. The religious atmosphere fills this book—Morley's *Life of Gladstone*—and blurs every outline. We are shown Mr Gladstone—note the 'Mister'—it's a touch of the trick—he wouldn't have said 'Mister Disraeli through a haze of reverence and Emerson and Marcus Aurelius' [and again I ask 'What is the matter with Marcus Aurelius?']. We begin to long for a little of the scepticism of precisely the age of Diderot, Rousseau and Voltaire. The heartless, irreverent, indecent eighteenth century produced the French Revolution. The age of Victoria produced—what?

Well, the 'age of Queen Victoria' (if one must personify so pedantic an abstraction) certainly did not produce anything like the French Revolution. *It* (if we may meet this trick of personification on its own mat) even stopped the menace of its violence—the Conciergerie, the Terror and its blood—stopped it by gradual steps and through various reformers fighting against odds. It effected a most evident if gradual improvement in the life of what used to be called 'the poor'. But I must not be entrapped into a defence of that abstraction, 'the Victorian Age'. If anyone here has a grudge against it for not having produced a colourable copy of the French Revolution of 1798, let him step outside and start making one. But on this Dallas (to continue with him) has some words to say worth your attention. He talks of Plutarch's *Lives* and fairly puts the fact that Plutarch's work, turning away from the stately, objective, method of Thucydides into biography, did actually coincide with the literary decadence of Greece. 'It must be borne in mind', says Plutarch in his Life of Alexander 'that my design is to write not Histories but Lives.' And the most glorious exploits are not always the most characteristic. Some-

THE CULT OF PERSONALITY

times a matter of less moment, an expression or a jest give a truer insight into a man's mind than the most famous sieges, the greatest armaments, the bloodiest battles.

There you have a plea for the biographical interpretation of history put by its earliest great practitioner, and put as well as it can ever be put. And when Lytton Strachey talks of Rousseau, Voltaire and others as prophets of the French Revolution, remind yourselves that when that Revolution broke nothing in Literature influenced its successive leaders comparably with Plutarch's *Lives*. At your peril, Gentlemen, help towards any despising of Greek, or at least the study of Hellenic thought, if for no other reason than that it happens to be irrepressible. It has twice come back; once to dismember a Pontificate and next a so-called Holy Empire. Hate it, despise it as you must; but beware of it. Let any nation beware of making Greek an outcast or an enemy.

VI

To return to our argument—I was pointing out that, however well managed, the business of treating history through a writer's own personality has its dangers. And if, as Aristotle held, poetry be more *philosophical* than history, telling us what an Agamemnon or an Oedipus (or if you will, by application, a Romeo or an Othello) did or suffered by rule of fate operating through event or character, as distinct from what Alcibiades actually did or suffered through interference or deflection of accidentals, why then, let us examine one or two of the foibles to which *expression* of one's own personality is prone.

(1) To begin with, we will start on an instinct, yours or mine. Few of us like a fellow who is full of himself. 'The world is so full of a number of things.'... It is also so full of such a number of *facts* we have no immediate use for, that I suppose in social life there is no greater bore than a well-informed man instructing you in anything you don't want to know, just here and now.

(2) Secondly, the insistent asserter of *opinion* derived from the introspective process may be an even greater nuisance. One hears of holy men in the East who spend life-times in the contemplation of their own stomachs: but (one would surmise) even so curious a rapture would have, despite fasting, to suffer doubt, if not disillusion, with the approach of middle-age.

(3) Thirdly, in Criticism too it makes for private arrogance and, through arrogance—which implies that its practitioner is thinking of himself and not of 'the other man' and his feelings—for tactlessness, offensiveness (though it be unconscious), in fine for Bad Manners. If, as Matthew Arnold reminds us somewhere, the only true *intellectual* process be Persuasion, how much more will it count in the general conduct of life, wherein the intellect is but one component, and no immoderately large one, in the priceless faculty of liking and being liked? Arrogance, too, has the defect of being provocative. When a critic's tone suggests that he has access to sources of inspiration denied to the rest of mankind and anyhow most certainly denied to *you*, the impulse is to hold him up on the frontier and ask to see

his passport: an opening that seldom leads to fruitful discussion on either side. Yet another defect in the self-centred critic—if it be another and separable from arrogance—is that his censure, even when just, conveys censoriousness, and his knowledge, even when sound, an air of condescension. Bacon puts this well and shrewdly. 'Knowledge', says he, 'be it in quantity more or less, if it be taken without the true corrective thereof, hath in it some nature of venom or malignity: and some effects of that venom, which is ventosity or swelling. The corrective spice, the mixture whereof maketh knowledge so sovereign, is Charity.' But the sweetest rebuke of censoriousness that ever came within my hearing was uttered by an ingenuous youth, an undergraduate, who probably to this day is unaware, would be even slightly alarmed to hear, that he had ever said a profound thing. He had listened for some time to a learned man, his senior, depreciating another senior, until fired at with 'But come, come: you *must* see that So-and-So is no good!' 'Well, sir', was the answer, 'I'm afraid I've always thought him rather a fine fellow: but of course *your* standard would be so high.'

Yes! and apart from the practice of Poetry and Criticism in print, even a too-intensive Self-Culture, remote from interest in the world and one's neighbours, may easily pass into a morose self-indulgence.

VII

Now if a man of my age may venture a criticism upon the Poetry and Fiction—the imaginative work in general—of to-day, I do find it, to me unpleasantly, tainted with this air of aloof condescension. I read it eagerly, though not in such quantity as youth could once devour if not digest: I am naturally often perplexed—as you may observe many a person of mature age to stand perplexed at a crossing where the motor traffic meets. Believe me, who have listened to many talks on this with Robert Bridges and more than one with Thomas Hardy, and been allowed to share in them, that I were a fool, and to myself an inconceivable one, without having learnt from much of their hope and trust in the young, to which my own heart urged. It might not be possible always to swallow Bridges' thunder that English poetry had exhausted old techniques and must invent new ones or perish; not possible always, for a man born sanguine, to grope with Hardy through a twilight between two worlds, one dead, the other powerless to be born. And yet, Hardy, like Sindbad entombed in the tale, descried the glimmer at the far end of the cave; both of these continued trusting in youth, as Meredith before them: and (be it observed) Hardy and Bridges—Charles Doughty too—each of those noble three attempted in old age, and achieved, a poem of large roll and sweep: poems, too, that trafficked with event and fate, with the beginnings of a nation, with the universal scheme of things.

Of course this derisive treatment of his characters by an author—or, when not derisive, patronising, and handling them as puppets—is no new thing, especially in our Fiction. It was habitual with Thackeray; habitual also though not openly confessed, with George Eliot. But I think it may be fairly said that to-day it pervades our

THE CULT OF PERSONALITY

later Fiction, or at any rate that part of it which calls for criticism. Perhaps, it may be as fairly said of our Poetry just now. In telling our tragic tales (and in large—to my thinking excessive—proportion they tend to tragedy) we have gone a long way beyond Aristotle's dictum that Tragedy concerns itself with the doings of men better or more eminent than ourselves; if indeed we have not reversed it. We deal by preference with sordid little lives. Is it through pity for them? or, as the tone more often suggests, through intellectual pride, assuming the God, hurting flies for our sport, watching them crawl? Or when the tone rises to anger—to inspired wrath if you will—and we get (to take a recent and notable instance) Mr Ezra Pound's *Draft of XXX Cantos*; a roomy thrice-heated oven into which he shovels, and in which he would shrivel, all men and things for which he has a righteous contempt. Is it a revolt against prettiness, convention, complacency? That is no new revolt, nor original. Go back a hundred years or so and we find Landor [who by the way warns us elsewhere that 'nothing is easier than to catch the air of originality'] protesting in an age adorned by Wordsworth, Coleridge, Shelley, that

> The satin slipper and the varnisht boot
> Encumber all the paths of Poesy,

and demanding Who can track a Grace's naked foot amid them all? Is it just a fashion of pessimism, or a real, seated pessimism in these dark uncertain days? If but a fashion, I would point out that Thomas Hardy, from whom many believe it to be derived, at least again and again finds tragedy (as Shakespeare did) in the nobility of his characters—Tess, Marty South, Gabriel Oak, the Mayor of Casterbridge—and by that illuminates the story. Or if it echo a genuine if angry acceptance of men's mood just now, cannot *some* poet lift up his eyes unto the hills whence cometh our help? At the worst, and as a stout writer—no quietist—wrote in his day:

We cannot steer our drifting raft, nor stem the resistless current; but we have it in our power to behave decently, to share the meagre stock of victuals fairly as long as they last, to take the good and evil as it comes, and even to hope, if we choose to do so, for a fair haven.

For my part I believe the raft can be steered, and that the Poet can give us eyes to sight land. In that faith, Gentlemen, I am speaking to you.

VIII

Yet, here, in this attempt to claim the poet's place as a citizen, let me get out of the way two possible misunderstandings. The first, a vulgar one, may be dismissed in a sentence or so. I do not urge any claim for him as a producer of obvious tribal, brass-band, so-called 'patriotic' verse. That sort of thing may have been useful, rightly stimulative among peoples in crises of their history. But the root of patriotism is not to be sought in strains like *Rule, Britannia!* These are not poetry, anyhow, and here do not concern us. Of such things, then, let so much be said.

Secondly, it is more important to get out of our minds that poetry *directly* inculcates any ethical doctrine. Matthew Arnold's talk about it as a Criticism of Life, if pressed into a definition, has almost every fault a definition can have. It is wider than a church door and narrower than a suicide. Poetry does, to be sure, criticise life in its way, but so does a Bow Street magistrate in his, and far more directly. The trouble here is that the poets themselves and their defenders have so often given us away by insinuating the true value of poetry under cover of something else—as something which leads to something else, something instructional, something useful. I fear that Horace himself falls into this fallacy, mixing up poetry's own function with the inappropriate function of practical utility; even as his contemporary, Strabo, tells us that the ancients held poetry to be a kind of elementary philosophy, pleasurably instructing us from childhood in character, behaviour and action. Surely (he argues) the Greeks did not teach their children poetry for the sake of sweetly influencing their souls, but rather for correcting their morals!

You all know how this nonsense of sugaring the powder with the jam persists into our own sixteenth-century criticism and well beyond it—with Webbe, with Puttenham, Harrington: how even our noble Sidney allowed his modesty to be over-awed by the pedantic tradition, the *reductio ad absurdum* of which we recognise in didactic poetry—*The Dispensary, The Botanic Garden*—that sort of thing. But of didactic poetry, again, let so much be said.

IX

Now where shall we find poetry's proper function?

My own suggestion is that we must go back well beyond much recent speculation in aesthetic, and rediscover it in the very old-fashioned doctrine of Harmony.

Let me try to explain this old doctrine, as I hold it, promising that, though you may deride my faith in it as simple, it is of gentle descent, since it derives from Plato, and not singular, since many have held it. For I imagine that many in youth have found it a 'conversion' to a light which no cross-winds of dogma or speculation have prevailed to extinguish. I hold, indeed, that any master secret of our Universe, if ever found, *must* be something vastly simple. But enough of personal apology.

By admission the immensity of this Universe staggers all imagination. It staggers even the reasoning of modern physicists or at least they seem to stagger one another's reason, as their reasonings certainly stagger an ordinary intelligence. Let me give you here the figure by which I sometimes try to bring this immensity home to my class in the *Poetics*. Suppose that I place in one corner of this lecture-room a marble to represent the earth, and in another a tennis ball for the sun, and that I scale down the diagonal to represent the distance between the earth and the sun—some ninety odd millions of miles. On that scale where do you suppose the *nearest* fixed star would lie? In the next street? Across by the Isle of Wight? It would lie somewhere near the Cape of Good Hope.

THE CULT OF PERSONALITY

And yet this immensity is not a chaos. (If it were, by the way, we should be unable to reason about it at all.) It stands and is perpetually renewed upon an ascertained harmony, so that, even as the tides on this planet, the great constellations themselves faint not in their watches, but move to their sentry posts and arrive to the predictable minute; this duty of obedience being of course that which Wordsworth hymns in his noble Ode,

Thou dost preserve the stars from wrong;
And the most ancient heavens, through Thee, are fresh and strong.

X

But in truth—a thought equally important for us and more consoling—this macrocosm of the Universe, with its harmony, cannot be apprehended at all except as it is focussed upon the eye and intelligence of man, the microcosm. Man, so far as we know, is the only audience at this tremendous concert, and the universal harmony meaningless and nothing to him save and in so far as he apprehends it by reference to some corresponding harmony in himself.

What is that corresponding harmony? Surmised of old and attempted to be explained by music of the spheres, by numbers, etc., it took out of surrounding ignorance strong confirmation for us as soon as Harvey discovered the secret of the circulation of the blood. Small specks as we are, we belong to the universe, and carry, almost all our time quite unconsciously, its rhythm within us. Indeed as a rule we are conscious of it only when we fall ill, when the heart beats irregularly, when the temperature flies up. But, over and above this corresponding physical rhythm, man has a native emotional impulse to merge himself in the greater harmony and be one with it: a spirit in his heart (as St Paul puts it) 'of adoption', 'the earnest expectation of the Creature', the yearning, the στοργή whereby we call *abba Father*. Now this most God-like of all human gifts—the singular gift separating man from the brutes —is *language*. If by language he can connect the music within himself with the great rhythm, he has disciplined himself to accord, and at the same time to feel pleasurably that he is in accord, with his Creator's purpose.

That I suggest is where the beneficent and proper function of poetry 'comes in'. That is why to the Greeks Apollo was equally and at once the god of poetry and the god of medicine; and in that I find, for my part, the duty of the poet as a citizen: by awaking his less sensitive fellows to an apprehension of the harmony beyond and yet within them, to help them to build the city of their habitation that it may be not only a 'dear City of Cecrops' but a 'dear City of Zeus'. That our poets may help us to build such a City!—

Movit Amphion lapides canendo.

XI

And, mind you, there is no detriment to the private soul in this service to the State and our fellow-citizens. Long ago Marcus Aurelius wrote—and as a Roman Emperor he should have known—

THE CULT OF PERSONALITY

Some seek for themselves private retiring-places, as country villages, sea-shores, mountains.... But this (thou must know) proceeds from an extravagant simplicity. For at what time soever thou wilt, it is in thy power to retire into thyself, dwelling within the walls of a city as on a sheepfold in the hills. And the true man is he who, mixing with his fellows, gently maintains the independence of his soul.

More than a hundred years ago when a long and weary war had brought, as long war always does, the wrong kind of man to the top, and Lord Eldon squatted upon a woolsack suppressing the liberties of Englishmen, Shelley demanded

> Oh, cease! must hate and death return?
> Cease! must men kill and die?

He appealed to the hearts of depressed, almost hopeless, contemporaries. But old men have told me, and reported how their fathers told them, how Shelley's appeal spoke to them and younger men, beating in their blood and inspiring hope of a better city as they dragged home (let us say) to their lodgings under the dismal lamps of Oxford Street. They had little voting power: yet insensibly that pulse in their blood commanded Parliament in the Palace of Westminster. 'And the land had peace forty years.' That is what on all evidence the vast majority of us to-day desire. Will no poet collect that flood, as song only can, and make the tide irresistible?

THE POET AS CITIZEN. III

TRADITION AND ORTHODOXY

I

IN FEBRUARY last we in England had our first opportunity of reading under the title *After Strange Gods: A Primer of Modern Heresy*, a series of three 'Page-Barbour' Lectures given by Mr T. S. Eliot before the University of Virginia. Anything written or spoken by Mr Eliot is eagerly awaited: and because his conclusions, if I accepted the premises, would strongly enforce, or by selected quotation might be used to enforce, some warnings I addressed to you the other day (and, as it happens, while he was speaking some thousands of miles away) against the prevalent individualism in modern writing, and the worship of originality for its own sake, as of an idol; I could be grateful for support so powerful, as in a degree I am. But the subject is to me a serious one; so serious that I should hate to invoke the support of any rhetorical enthymemes which seem unsound to me, or to use such for my purpose on any man's *ipse dixit*, whatever my esteem for the man himself. And so I shall take leave, this morning, to question some two or three of Mr Eliot's pronouncements.

II

He, to be sure, in his Preface very frankly disclaims and rejects argument.

'I am not arguing or reasoning', he says, 'or engaging in controversy with those whose views are radically opposed to such as mine. In our time controversy seems to me, on really fundamental matters, to be futile. It can only usefully be practised where there is a common understanding. It requires common assumptions, and perhaps the assumptions that are only felt are more important than those that can be formulated. The acrimony which accompanies much debate is a symptom of difference so large that there is nothing to argue about. We experience such profound differences with some of our contemporaries that the nearest parallel is the difference between one epoch and another. In a society like ours, worm-eaten with Liberalism, the only thing possible for a person of strong convictions is to state a point of view and leave it at that.'

Now this, reduced to plain terms, amounts to no more than 'I am not arguing with you: I am just telling you'. It takes up an attitude which, however politely assumed, I find hard to differentiate from that of Thrasymachus in the *Republic*; who (if you remember) having drenched his audience with a pailful of his own opinions on Justice, was for 'leaving it at that' and walking off, when Socrates plucked him by the sleeve 'O Thrasymachus, excellent man, how suggestive are your remarks! And are you really going to move away before you have fairly taught or learned whether they are true or not?' Mr Eliot's is, at any rate, the attitude of a dogmatist: and in one who is addressing (as he announces) the 'possibly convertible' about the least likely to succeed:

since, the 'convertible' being by hypothesis unregenerate as yet; and since in my experience the unregenerate, if intelligent at all, are prone to ask questions; any claim or suspicion of a claim that you have access to wells of inspiration denied to the rest of mankind is apt to repel at the start.

I am particularly sorry that a critic so finely equipped as Mr Eliot, and just now possessed of so much influence, should be in successive books so evidently hardening into this oracular attitude, because I feel sure that it can only end in ossification. Already, while elaborately endeavouring to define tradition and orthodoxy, to separate them, in practice he is mixing them up, and confusing both with religion and politics. And I am the sorrier over these lectures of his because, when talking of tradition, he sharpens and betters many points I tried to put to you, Gentlemen, in a couple of lectures last Michaelmas Term on 'The Poet as Citizen'. Up to a point I am greatly his debtor for the improvement: and if at that point I must part company with him I shall, before we part to-day, submit my reasons.

III

Since his concept of Orthodoxy concerns me less than his concept of Tradition—though it puzzles me more—let us, for our present purpose, first get that conception cleared out of the way, if we can.

It puzzles me more because while careful, and even more than careful, to define what he means by Tradition, when he comes to Orthodoxy he seems to me to wander around the word without fixing it at all until

TRADITION AND ORTHODOXY 47

we come to his third and last lecture. In the first he gives it a 'similar inclusiveness' with Tradition, and proceeds 'though of course I believe that a right tradition for us must be also a Christian tradition, and that Orthodoxy in general implies Christian orthodoxy, I do not propose to lead the present series of lectures to a theological conclusion'. Yet after a dozen words he dives off into an attack on liberalism in Church and politics with illustrative quotations, the worth of which I shall presently examine.

The interposed sentence, or half-sentence, runs— 'The relation between tradition and orthodoxy in the past is evident enough'. But 'the past', so used, is surely the vaguest of terms. For example, Orthodoxy *in the past*, before and after the Council of Trent—before and after 1563, its last sitting—carried for Catholic Europe two very different meanings: the newer one restricting it in sundry ways and fencing the restrictions with anathema. Up to that date the Medieval Church had been moving. For a single instance—Many of its churchmen hitherto allowed as orthodox did not receive as canonical all the Apocrypha or accept with an equal devotion the Second Book of Maccabees with St Mark's Gospel. As my friend Mr Bernard Manning has put it—

> The Roman Church after the sixteenth century was less corrupt, freer from scandals, more devoted to its spiritual work, more efficient in its administration; but it was less free intellectually, less bold, in all its uses of the Christian tradition, more fearful of exploring into the unsearchable riches of Christ, than it had been before the Council of Trent. It definitely refused to

carry with it into modern times some part of its ancient and medieval heritage. This happened partly from reaction against Protestantism.

Well, but after the Reformation what happens to Orthodoxy under Protestantism? We find one Orthodoxy narrowing itself into the Lutheran, another (fiercely) in the Calvinistic Church. A third, through the polemics of the seventeenth century, despite the gentle efforts and gentle examples in living of such men as Herbert, Jeremy Taylor and the Cambridge Platonists, economised its allowance of Orthodoxy to the Church of England in the eighteenth century—an Orthodoxy in part political, in part asleep on formularies, in spirit inert, in daily practice lazy, choleric only when some intrusive evangelist rang the bell disturbing the afternoon doze: while—to infringe with respect upon Mr Eliot's native soil—scarcely had the Pilgrim Fathers landed on Plymouth Rock before they started to build an Orthodoxy of their own at least as repressive and rigidly tyrannous as anything they had fled from. Escaping across the Atlantic for liberty of conscience, they found a New England, cast there the anchor of their souls, landed, and ran to and fro burning 'witches'.

I am sorry to have been led even so far as this into ecclesiastical story: but Mr Eliot's method so far compels me. For in my search after what he means by Orthodoxy in literature I find him continually sliding off into theology. Pursuing, I learn that a *Tradition*, in so far as it differs from Orthodoxy, is a way of feeling and acting which characterises a group throughout generations; and that it must largely be, or that many of the elements in it must be, unconscious—and here I do not think Mr Eliot will quarrel with me if I interpret this a little more definitely as 'good manners inherited through breeding', 'manners' as a term carrying just that moral significance which William of Wykeham intended and bequeathed in his noble motto *Manners makyth Man*';—'whereas', Mr Eliot proceeds, 'the maintenance of Orthodoxy is a matter which calls for the exercise of all our conscious intelligence'. The *maintenance*, then, will be conscious; but Orthodoxy itself 'exists, whether realised in anyone's thought or not'. Orthodoxy, again, is 'continuous'; and yet, in Mr Eliot's words, 'a whole generation might conceivably pass without orthodox thought, or, as by Athanasius, Orthodoxy may be upheld by one man against the world'. These sayings, dropped in the course of a spoken lecture, must have puzzled his audience somewhat; and merely dropped and 'left at that' they *are* puzzling, though not irreconcilable. Still pursuing, I come, in his third and last lecture, to a pronouncement clear enough. 'What I have been leading up to', he says, 'is the following assertion: that when morals cease to be a matter of tradition and orthodoxy—that is, of the habits of the community formulated, corrected and elevated by the continuous thought and direction of the Church—and when each man is to elaborate his own, then *personality* becomes a thing of alarming importance.'

[But has it ever been less, in human history?]

IV

Now let me be equally definite in taking up the separate parts of the above composite assertion. I agree, of course, that 'when morals cease to be a matter of tradition... and when each man is to elaborate his own, then personality becomes a thing of alarming importance'. It was this, and just this, I was trying to preach to you in my lectures before Christmas on 'The Poet as Citizen'; and if Mr Eliot uses the tone of authority while I can only attempt persuasion, I must be the more indebted to authority for his backing.

But when he goes on to insist that Tradition requires to be 'formulated, corrected, and elevated by the continuous thought and direction of the Church', I must cry halt.

To begin with, I doubt if the tradition of any community can ever be 'formulated'—if even its minor unconscious habits can be 'formulated' save in books of etiquette, the rules of which for one generation tend to be a laughing-stock for the next. (Should a man for example wear his hat at table when dining with the King?) But tradition more vital—tradition in matters which deeply concern the moral, physical, intellectual health of a society—is at once too various and too delicate a thing to be caught, constricted within formulas or creeds by any Church. Take, for instance, Poetry; with which and its traditions we have been specially concerned. When, as a historical fact, have the traditions of Poetry been usefully formulated, or even, with the great exception of Dante, considerably directed, by any Church? Elevated by religious fervour Poetry may be, of course, and often has been; as by other passionate convictions theologically orthodox or unorthodox in their day. The real answer to Mr Eliot's question 'Why is most religious verse so bad?' is, I should contend, precisely in so far as it has submitted to his own theory. He accounts for it by the ingenious suggestion that people who write devotional verse are usually writing as they want to feel rather than as they do feel. I rather believe the great mass of what is called in editorial offices 'Vicarage Verse' to be quite sincere, and bad only because the people who write it are not poets. Poetry in short is Poetry: it has known many creeds and survived them all. One after another they have discredited and cast down his altars, but Apollo survives. Whoso would recruit him from one category into another is mixing up things that differ: whoso would enslave him to any flock, be it of Admetus or of the Archbishop of Canterbury, is weaving nets for the wind.

V

But to pass over many questions raised by this claim that 'the Church' should exercise control over our Literature, and over Poetry in particular—as for example the question put to Dogberry 'How if a will not?' and if so, how punishable, and by whom? We come to the fatal question '*What and which Church?*'

Well, we know from previous declarations of his creed or creeds in religion and politics how Mr Eliot would like this to be answered. And here I must simply say that, as I read it, Literature in England has never in fact submitted to a control so narrow, and (in my hope and belief) never will.

I am sorry, I repeat, to have been dragged by him even so far into the confines of dogmatic theology: but his views of right Literature and his illustrations constantly slide off into that; as, to do him justice, they logically must. And, if I may say it without acrimony, those views seem to be largely coloured by a particular hatred of what he calls Liberalism: and I must most seriously protest against the device by which, to present the Liberalism of a century ago, he imposes upon a foreign audience, presumably unacquainted with the story he is telling, a passage of invective by a writer whose name, if not wholly forgotten, any serious critic to-day would either pass over as negligible among the great antagonists, or select only as a curiosity of forgotten spite. This is how Mr Eliot adduces his testimony—'There was certainly (he says), a hundred years ago, a relation between the Liberalism which attacked the Church and the Liberalism which appeared in politics'. According to a contemporary, William Palmer, the former group of Liberals—

'Were eager to eliminate from the Prayer-book the belief in the Scriptures, the Creeds, the worship of Christ. They called for the admission of Unitarian infidels as fellow-believers. They would eviscerate the Prayer-book, reduce the Articles to a few deistic formularies, and reduce religion to a state of anarchy and confusion', etc.

'It is well to remember', adds Mr Eliot, 'that this sort of Liberalism was flourishing a century ago; it is also well to remember that it is flourishing still.'

VI

But fair and softly! Who was this William Palmer, whose denunciation of the Liberals in 1843 Mr Eliot tosses before an audience in Virginia, U.S.A. as true contemporary description, capped by his own *ipse dixit* that 'this sort of Liberalism is flourishing still'? The short footnote in his printed lecture says merely 'Quoted in *Northern Catholicism*, p. 9'. I look up that work (a collection of Anglo-Catholic papers) and find on p. 9 the passage just quoted as testimony, and again 'left at that'. Pursuing, I get at the works of William Palmer, and some contemporary evidence concerning him. He was, admittedly, a very learned man, an Irishman, a violent Anti-papist: who, coming across to Oxford, latish, considerably helped the beginnings of what is called the Oxford Movement by his liturgical information. 'But', says Newman after a tribute to his gifts, 'he was deficient in depth, and besides'—you must forgive me, Gentlemen—the words are Newman's, not mine—'coming from a distance, he had never really grown into an Oxford man'. In brief he was impracticable, positive, irascible as a bull at a hint of the Scarlet Woman: and his methods of controversy invited rebuke for themselves in a pamphlet attributed to M. Renouf and politely, beyond their worth, condescended to by Hurrell Froude. I have studied the work from which Mr Eliot took his quotation at second-hand (*Narrative of Events connected with 'Tracts for the Times'*), and, if you have not guessed it from the very style of the quotation, can only add that his arguments strike me as those of a learned but rather vulgar disputant, originally by nature, provincially by habit, deficient in self-control.

Now had it not been fairer if Mr Eliot, addressing in Virginia, U.S.A. an audience presumably unacquainted with the story of this eccentric cleric, had quoted against the Liberalism of a hundred years ago the testimony of its foremost contemporary opponent; a voice infinitely more authoritative, a book not only accessible, but now classical? I mean, of course, Newman and his *Apologia*. It had surely been more to his right purpose to take the famous note on 'Liberalism' towards the end of that book. I invite you, Gentlemen, to read the whole of Newman's note, the manner of which I have here but time to illustrate by a few sentences.

When [says Newman] in the beginning of the present century [that is, the last century] after many years of moral and intellectual declension, the University of Oxford woke up to a sense of its duties, and began to reform itself, the first instruments of this change, to whose zeal and courage we all owe so much, were naturally thrown together for mutual support, against the numerous obstacles which lay in their path, and soon stood out in relief from the body of residents, who, though many of them men of talent themselves, cared little for the object which the others had at heart. These Reformers, as they may be called, were for some years members of scarcely more than three or four Colleges; and their own Colleges, as being under their direct influence, of course had the benefit of those stricter views of discipline and teaching, which they themselves were urging on the University. They had, in no long time, enough of real progress in their several spheres of exertion, and enough of reputation out of doors, to warrant them in considering themselves the élite of the place.

TRADITION AND ORTHODOXY

Thus was formed an intellectual circle or class in the University,—men, who felt they had a career before them, as soon as the pupils, whom they were forming, came into public life; men, whom non-residents, whether country parsons or preachers of the Low Church, on coming up from time to time to the old place, would look at, partly with admiration, partly with suspicion, as being an honour indeed to Oxford, but withal exposed to the temptation of ambitious views, and to the spiritual evils signified in what is called the 'pride of reason'.

Nor was this imputation altogether unjust; for, as they were following out the proper idea of a University, of course they suffered more or less from the moral malady incident to such a pursuit. The very object of such great institutions lies in the cultivation of the mind and the spread of knowledge: if this object, as all human objects, has its dangers at all times, much more would these exist in the case of men, who were engaged in a work of reformation, and had the opportunity of measuring themselves, not only with those who were their equals in intellect, but with the many who were below them. In this select circle or class of men, in various Colleges, the direct instruments and the choice fruit of real University Reform, we see the rudiments of the Liberal party.

Now Newman's main argument may be right or may be wrong. But I invite you, remembering that the above sentences were penned by one who had already admitted—to use his own words—that 'From the age of fifteen dogma has been the fundamental principle of my religion: I know no other sort of religion: cannot enter into any other sort of religion'—I invite you to contrast that passage, simply as an example of style in controversy with that other quotation from Mr William Palmer, and then turn to these few of Newman's own words from his well-known 'Definition of a Gentleman'—

If he engages in controversy of any kind, his disciplined intellect preserves him from the blundering discourtesy of better, though less educated minds; who, like blunt weapons, tear and hack instead of cutting clean, who mistake the point in argument, waste their strength on trifles, and leave the question more involved than they found it. He may be right or wrong in his opinion, but he is too clear-headed to be unjust: he is as simple as he is forcible, and as brief as he is decisive.

It is—as a lawyer would say—'not for me to advise'. Yet I think, in Mr Eliot's place and with his intention, I should have chosen to prefer and present Newman before W. Palmer as a descriptive writer.

VII

But when Mr Eliot speaks of Tradition I am grateful to him; and the more beholden because, in a voice that carries far beyond mine and in a tone I could not imitate, he was uttering to his audience in Virginia the very caution that I was suggesting here to you—and, as it happened, at the very moment; a warning, that is, and a protest, against the exploitation of self, the intrusion of an author's 'personality' or 'individuality' upon his work; an egoism of late years in fashion, accepted and applauded by critics, by many if not most as a merit in itself, by some as even the first of merits: my contention being rather that in writing as in other arts—as evidently as in social life—self-assertiveness almost infallibly suggests some defect of breeding. In a familiar 'essay', to be sure, a man may unbosom himself; the more pardonably in proportion as his confessions are worth while. But the familiar essay is a delicate business demanding

TRADITION AND ORTHODOXY

a curious tact of its own: and success in it carries no warrant for use in larger spheres of writing—in epic, tragedy, history or the novel. In these the true writer (if I may put it vulgarly) sticks to his job, is immersed in it, and lets his 'personality' take care of itself—which it will certainly do whether he forget it or even, should he be writing history, take pains to exclude it. Consider Thucydides, for example. He begins 'Thucydides an Athenian composed an account of the war between the Peloponnesians and the Athenians. He considered from the beginning that such an account would be valuable.' Thenceforward we have an austere narrative, bone-bare even when he himself was mixed up in the events and condemned for failure. He allows no pause for justification or self-excuse. Still in its stride the detailed unemotional inflexible narrative moves on to the terrible climax in the caves of Syracuse—this, even, told austerely. *Then* we realise the whole composition as at once true and a work of art; *then* the power suppressed, the genius commanding it and at length disclosed, the man as characteristic, a giant among historians.

Holding this poor opinion of self-assertiveness obtruding upon art, I was heartened, of course, on reading such passages as these in Mr Eliot's lectures:

> The general effect in literature of the lack of any strong tradition is twofold: extreme individualism in views, and no accepted rules or opinions as to the limitations of the literary job.

That and

> It is true that the existence of a right tradition, simply by its influence upon the environment in which the poet develops, will tend to restrict eccentricity to manageable limits: but it is not

even by the lack of this restraining influence that the absence of tradition is most deplorable. What is disastrous is that the writer should deliberately give rein to his 'individuality'; that he should even cultivate his differences from others; and that his readers should cherish the author of genius, not in spite of his deviations from the inherited wisdom of the race, but because of them.

Well, this passage might stand as text before some arguments of mine. But there was one which lack of time compelled me to shorten; and I am glad of this opportunity to recall it with a little more insistence: for it concerns a prevalent temper among writers of to-day in most forms of creative work, and in criticism too.

You may or may not remember my inviting your attention to one trap among several baited for artists and critics by this worm of personality—this *eidolon omphalou*, as I may call it. I mean the lure toward self-conceit; expressed in practice by condescension, writing down to one's audience, or (worse) choosing an ignoble subject and writing down to that. On this pretentiousness in contemporary criticism I shall not here dwell. Even when Delphi claimed to be the whole world's navel the voice of Apollo disguised itself in ambiguity, through smoke. With a score or two of Pythians each drawing inspiration from the centre of his own unbelted personality, the hum of the Oracles passes into a noise not less hideous because confused and dissipated.

But for lack of time I must hasten past the critics and come to writers engaged just now upon creative work, whether in Poetry or Fiction: for these after all are the primary ones in any important age. Whether it belong

TRADITION AND ORTHODOXY

to post-war disillusionment, or to a curious deflection of our old aristocratic tradition in literature to adapt itself to democracy and instinctively to patronise it —more or less in the style of a grand lady opening a Women's Institute—I think that few students of contemporary poems and novels will deny the almost universal tendency of such writers as this generation has seriously taken, to choose unheroic themes, sordid environments, characters to be dangled as marionettes from aloft and condescendingly explained through commentary.

I shall not ask you to take any assurance of mine about that sort of thing as being about the easiest scamping of real art and to that extent contemptible, however popular. I prefer to quote here a passage I came upon, a few weeks ago, in *The Spectator*. A reviewer, Mr H. E. Bates, wrote thus of a certain novel

> [The writer] is not a great writer but a precious one. His attitude throughout the book is one of superiority. Whereas the great writer credits the reader with an intelligence equal to his own, the lesser writer credits him with less; the great writer keeps himself detached and unseen, never stepping between himself and the picture; but the lesser writer keeps holding himself up, Sir Oracle fashion, with what he considers are vital explanations or remarks of profound philosophical importance.

It may seem pedantic to enforce this by going back to Aristotle and his insistence on nobility of character ($\tau\grave{o}$ $\beta\epsilon\lambda\tau\acute{\iota}o\nu$) as a necessary appanage of the true Tragic Hero. But consider Shakespeare's tragic heroes, and how even their enemies salute them, dead. Recall Antony's grand words over the corpse of Brutus, with Octavius' echo of them: recall Antony's own last claim

>   a Roman by a Roman
> Valiantly vanquish'd—

and Octavius' *coda* over him and Cleopatra—

> No grave upon the earth shall clip in it
> A pair so famous. High events as these
> Strike those that make them: and their story's
> No less in pity than his glory which
> Brought them to be lamented.

Even poor Timon ends as noble Timon; for Coriolanus the drums are bidden to beat, the pikes to be trailed, for

> the most noble corse that ever herald
> Did follow to his urn.

So, of Hamlet—

> Let four captains
> Bear Hamlet, like a soldier, to the stage;
> ...and, for his passage,
> The soldiers' music and the rites of war
> Speak loudly for him.

That is the accent by which great writers communicate their magnanimity and teach the rest of us that 'we are greater than we know'.

VIII

I have dwelt at some length on this particular tendency of ego-worship; to belittle the author's theme, patronise his subject, parade what in himself is what an Athenian would have called 'the idiotic', and to hang (if I may

TRADITION AND ORTHODOXY

adapt a phrase of Henry James') our frail humanity as a beaten rag upon a clothes-line: and have dwelt on this vice, among traps of egoism indicated in my last lecture, because in proportion to its prevalence just now we should thank Mr Eliot alike for his vigour and his opportuneness in denouncing it.

But I do not thank him for the rhetorical sleight of hand or series of ambiguities by which he palms off this ego-worship as identical with 'Liberalism'. We must remember, of course—and the more vividly for his insistence upon the indelibility of early training—that he is a New Englander addressing an audience in America's conservative South, whose prejudices on a local issue he starts, as a converted missionary, to enlist for his general attack on what he calls 'Liberalism'. What he means by 'Liberalism', except that it is something he dislikes, one must use patience to discern, so dexterously he shuffles religion into politics, politics into literature, tradition into dogma, to and fro, until the reader—let alone a listener—can scarcely tell out of what category the card (so to speak) is being dealt. Still if one keeps gripping, as Menelaus and his comrades did upon the Old Man of the Sea, this may be squeezed out—that 'Liberalism' is anything which questions dogma: which dogma, to be right dogma, is the priestly utterance of a particular offset of a particular branch of a historically fissiparous Church.

IX

Well, as Mr Eliot wisely hints in the course of his lectures, we can none of us escape the shadow of what we learned at our mother's knee. And as my own *Alma Mater* insisted (perhaps too austerely) upon Logic, I find it hard to call myself off from such a roaring scent after the fallacy of the 'Undistributed Middle' as he here puts up. But perhaps the simplest way to go to work is to define what Liberalism means to *me*. Whether you agree or not, we come to a point, and so our business is advanced.

I define 'Liberalism', then, first as a *habit of mind*. This at once disengages it from formulas, party cries, vestments or 'shirts' in religion or politics. It is neither a separate stick nor a faggot of opinions out of which, if one be dropped, brand and faggot be involved together and cast as heretical to the fire.

Further, it is a habit of mind which exercises, and claims to exercise, man's right, on this planet in this mysterious universe, surrounded on all hands by ignorance, to lift some veil of that curtain if he can: in short, to think for himself. As I see it, a man owes that effort to his own dignity as well as to the help of his fellows. But at any rate that effort must find itself—as Columbus found it at Salamanca before he could start on discovering the outpost of Mr Eliot's nativity—in direct opposition to dogmatic clerical assurance that there was not, nor could be, any such place.

And—yet further—let me say that this claim for the free operation of man's mind has been, if you will con-

TRADITION AND ORTHODOXY

sider it, Gentlemen, the fount and inspiration of the greatest literature bequeathed through centuries to civilised Europe—and our inheritance yet to be nursed in increase, not for our sake alone (since charity lies at its emotional base), but for others until the comity of Europe recover its balance. Go further back than Plato if you will: but start, if you will, with Plato and the dogmas upon which his thought operated for enlightenment. Follow Literature down—But no! What has Newman himself, the fairest upholder of dogma, to admit of the Western world's literature?—

He must confess, surveying it in a series of *Lectures to the Roman Catholic University of Ireland*, that the contribution of dogmatic writers to it has been negligible: in Italy, France, England alike—all but null. He faces the admission of England that 'a literature, when it is formed, is a national and historical fact; it is a matter of the past and the present, and can be as little ignored as the present, as little undone as the past'. If his co-religionists have to build a new literature upon dogma, they must start upon a new one. And who, reviewing the great names in our own Literature, however curiously, can hold that as a solid phalanx they do not stand for this free play of the human mind?—Chaucer, Langland, Spenser, Shakespeare [I dare say I may claim through age and circumstance, to have heard as much as any of you to Shakespeare's discredit, while never yet that he was illiberal], Milton, Dryden, Blake, Coleridge, Shelley, Byron, Landor; Bacon, Locke, Berkeley, Newton, Butler, Darwin; Fielding, Johnson, Scott, Dickens.... Which of these do we not connect, as part of our indebtedness to them, with the unhampered play, imaginative or strictly 'scientific', of man's mind?

And so—and if we read the story right—this 'Liberalism' which Mr Eliot arraigns as a worm, eating into the traditions of our society, reveals itself rather as Tradition itself, throughout Literature (which is Thought worth setting down and recording) the organic spirit persisting, aërating, preserving, the liberties our ancestors won and we inherit.

X

All great principles have their risks: else they were not worth fighting for. No one disputes that a man's liberty to think his own thoughts and express them in words can be abused, even as the Liberty of the Press is daily abused among us: that it may be pleaded as condoning, if not justifying, much that is eccentric, even frantic. Such is the price; and in this world the inestimable jewel of Freedom can only be had at a price. For my part I cannot see how anyone can study our English Literature—for six centuries now a 'glory of our blood and state' and yet a most 'substantial thing' —without feeling that in his blood and state this liberty of thought is not only a tradition but its dominant tradition, web and woof; or mistrust the sleight that would pass it off on us for bastard, as a sophism offending fact, repulsive to intelligence. I turn to Milton—

> Fool! he sees not the firm root out of which we all grow, though into branches.

TRADITION AND ORTHODOXY

Here, in this your University, the field of our literature is spread before you for your judgment. To that I leave it, reminding you only that Milton and Wordsworth were her sons who is now your mother: that Milton wrote this—

> Lords and commons of England, consider what nation it is whereof ye are and whereof ye are the governors; a nation... not beneath the reach of any point that human capacity can soar to.

and Wordsworth—

> We must be free or die, who speak the tongue
> That Shakespeare spake: the faith and morals hold
> Which Milton held—

Trite words: but as true to-day and imperative as when they were written! For—and to conclude—What is the alternative? What the dirty trump card ever up dogma's sleeve to be slid down and sneaked, upon opportunity? It is suppression; tyranny (as Pascal defined it 'the determination to get in that way what you cannot in another'); in its final brutal word—force. Look around Europe to-day and consider under what masks dogma is not feeling for, or openly shaking, this weapon to cow the minds of free men; and ask yourselves if it be not the inherited duty of our race to vindicate the tradition of that Liberty which was the ark within the citadel of our fathers' souls.

FIRST AID IN CRITICISING. I

ON BEING DEFINITE

INTRODUCTORY

WE were gathered, once upon a time, in the rooms of the late Dr Henry Jackson of Trinity—remembered by many for their hospitality with large discourse; and someone had started a bright new theory of Poetry, based (I think) on admiration of a recent volume by Francis Thompson. The talk veered this way and that with winds of doctrine and no more promise of fixity than one expects of such disputes, when one of the party appealed to Jackson. 'Oh, if you ask me', said Jackson, reaching for his tobacco-jar, 'I am content to take Poetry as the stuff the poets have written.'

I

I shall take, Gentlemen, that observation by a wise man as at once the text of one or two elementary lectures and my *apologia* for them. You may object at once that it narrows their scope: that in their concern with the concrete and with practicality (if they can attain it) they must needs deny themselves, and deny you, much delight in speculative Aesthetic. Well you must discover, as we go along, if I am ignorant of that delight or am callous to it.

But my purpose, perhaps, may be illustrated by

ON BEING DEFINITE

comparing and contrasting three separate passages (each good in its way) from *Biographia Literaria*—that monument of noble criticism festooned with irrelevance and the poppy.

In the first extract Coleridge is dealing the *coup de grâce* to David Hartley's theory of the Association of Ideas or (to speak more accurately) he dislocates and throws aside the mainspring of Hartley's mechanical theory. Coleridge writes—

We will pass by the utter incompatibility of such a law (if law it may be called, which would itself be the slave of chances) with even that appearance of rationality forced upon us by the outward phaenomena of human conduct, abstracted from our own consciousness. We will agree to forget this for the moment, in order to fix our attention on that subordination of final to efficient causes in the human being, which flows of necessity from the assumption, that the will and, with the will, all acts of thought and attention are parts and products of this blind mechanism, instead of being distinct powers, whose function it is to control, determine, and modify the phantasmal chaos of association. The soul becomes a mere *ens logicum*; for, as a real separable being, it would be more worthless and ludicrous than the Grimalkins in the Cat-harpsichord, described in the *Spectator*. For these did form a part of the process; but, in Hartley's scheme, the soul is present only to be pinched or stroked, while the very squeals or purring are produced by an agency wholly independent and alien.

I curtail the paragraph here. This much of it suffices to serve us; and Coleridge's pre-eminent gifts included no monitory sense, or but a faint one, of the full-stop.

My second passage I take from Chapter 14 of the *Biographia*—a famous one, summarising in the 'Perfect Poet' that prime and principal quality of Imagination towards defining which, with breaks and hesitations, he had been tortuously working. 'The Poet', he writes,

described in *ideal* perfection—brings the whole soul of man into activity with the subordination of its faculties to each other, according to their relative worth and dignity. He diffuses a tone and spirit of unity, that blends, and (as it were) *fuses*, each into each, by that synthetic and magical power, to which we have exclusively appropriated the name of imagination. This power, first put in action by the will and understanding, and retained under their irremissive, though gentle and unnoticed, controul (*laxis effertur habenis*) reveals itself in the balance or reconciliation of opposite or discordant qualities: of sameness, with difference; of the general, with the concrete; the idea, with the image; the individual, with the representative; the sense of novelty and freshness, with old and familiar objects; a more than usual state of emotion, with more than usual order; judgement ever awake and steady self-possession, with enthusiasm and feeling profound or vehement; and while it blends and harmonizes the natural and the artificial, still subordinates art to nature; the manner to the matter; and our admiration of the poet to our sympathy with the poetry.

For my third passage I go to Chapter 17 and choose a piece of particular criticism directed upon Wordsworth's *The Thorn*. You all know the poem, I assume: the tale of a cheated woman who in madness does away with her child born out of wedlock. Wordsworth (who, by the way, had no need in such a story to draw heavily upon his imagination) had thought it necessary to preface the poem with a conscientious defence of its diction. He is not (he says) telling the story in his own words, but putting it into the mouth of a supposed narrator: and of what kind of narrator 'the Reader will perhaps have a general notion if he has ever known a

ON BEING DEFINITE

man, a Captain of a small trading vessel for example, who, being past the middle age of life, had retired upon an annuity or small independent income to some village or country town of which he was not a native or in which he had not been accustomed to live. Such men, having little to do, become credulous and talkative from indolence', etc.

Now Coleridge (I need not remind you) had had some practice of his own with a retired Mariner, in making him speak poetically. And when Wordsworth makes *his* Mariner speak poetically, Coleridge is generous, as of the lines

> At all times of the day and night
>   This wretched woman thither goes;
> And she is known to every star
>   And every wind that blows....

Only he notes how little consonant this is with Wordsworth's pet claim to be using the language of ordinary men and women. 'And I reflect with delight', he adds, 'how little a mere theory, though of his own workmanship, interferes with the processes of genuine imagination in a man of true poetic genius who possesses, as Mr Wordsworth, if ever man did, most assuredly does possess,   The Vision and the Faculty divine.'

When, however, Wordsworth does make his supposed narrator talk in language flat enough for any man, with or without a small annuity, telling of the pond beside his tree of tragedy—

> I've measured it from side to side;
> 'Tis three feet long, and two feet wide.

Coleridge very justly smiles at this and other lapses in the poem as 'sudden and unpleasant sinkings'. (Wordsworth, though nettled, cut out the lines and substituted others, dull enough but less calculated to excite derision.) But Coleridge, having put his finger on the particular, proceeds to a sound generalisation upon it; and so brings me to my third extract.

> Every man's language has, first, its *individualities*; secondly, the common properties of the *class* to which he belongs; and thirdly, words and phrases of *universal* use. The language of Hooker, Bacon, Bishop, Taylor, and Burke differs from the common language of the learned class only by the superior number and novelty of the thoughts and relations which they had to convey. The language of Algernon Sidney differs not at all from that, which every well-educated gentleman would wish to write, and (with due allowances for the undeliberateness, and less connected train, of thinking natural and proper to conversation) such as he would wish to talk. Neither one nor the other differ half so much from the general language of cultivated society, as the language of Mr Wordsworth's homeliest composition differs from that of a common peasant. For 'real' therefore, we must substitute *ordinary*, or *lingua communis*. And this, we have proved, is no more to be found in the phraseology of low and rustic life than in that of any other class. Omit the peculiarities of each, and the result of course must be common to all. And assuredly the omissions and changes to be made in the language of rustics, before it could be transferred to any species of poem, except the drama or other professed imitation, are at least as numerous and weighty, as would be required in adapting to the same purpose the ordinary language of tradesmen and manufacturers. Not to mention, that the language so highly extolled by Mr Wordsworth varies in every county, nay in every village, according to the accidental character of the clergyman, the existence or non-existence of schools; or even, perhaps, as the

exciseman, publican, or barber, happen to be, or not to be, zealous politicians, and readers of the weekly newspaper *pro bono publico*. Anterior to cultivation, the *lingua communis* of every country, as Dante has well observed, exists every where in parts, and no where as a whole.

II

I have quoted to you, Gentlemen, three passages, all of which in their several ways do Coleridge credit.

But mark the difference, for our purpose.

(*a*) In the first he is engaged in destroying a theory of Aesthetic which, fashionable in its day, had been in his day important for him, but is now not only dead (mainly through his killing) but superimposed by the corpses of several later theories. 'Association of Ideas' (as I hope we shall see, later on) must lie at the root of poetical composition. For us, Coleridge is flogging, in Hartley, a dead horse, or 'stroking', to borrow his own image, 'a *caput mortuum*.' He does it, while effectually, very gently: and this, as I think, not because the revered David Hartley had been a Fellow, in this University, of his own Jesus College—that hot-bed of ideas! 'I gave his name to my first-born', writes Coleridge; and, what is more, he remembered to be there and do it at the font. 'A great man, a great thinker', he calls Hartley; but in truth if one has 'to lay hands on his father Parmenides', Coleridge's way with Hartley is Coleridge's way in general and a model yet for us all, albeit assuredly not in its woolly phrasing.

But, apart from its value as a model of temper in controversy—of so handling a destructive argument that you make it fatal, technical yet keep it mannerly—any interest that survives nowadays in our first passage can be but historical or biographical; historical if we choose to study the evolutions of aesthetic theory, biographical if we are concerned in tracing Coleridge's own mental development. To concern us with this, indeed, was the professed purpose of the *Biographia*, as its name denotes. It is also the reason why so very large a proportion of what is permanently valuable in the *Biographia* will be found in its digressions and 'asides'. Here, and for *our* purpose at any rate, we are no more concerned with Hartley and his speculations than with any of those more ancient yet transient systems of philosophy embalmed in the pages of Ritter and Preller.

(*b*) Of the second passage, deservedly so famous, I shall have something to say in another lecture: but nothing for the moment except to warn you that 'Imagination' is an abstract term and, like other abstract terms, may easily mislead you—even after you have defined it—into using it to mean more than it means: as Mr Richards in his *Principles of Literary Criticism* has pointed out that it misled Coleridge himself. Let us then, while admitting the passage to be finely constructive, as that on Hartley was destructive, leave it for the present and consider Coleridge's observation on *The Thorn*.

(*c*) Here he is saying definitely what he thinks of a definite poem and of definite lines in it. And I commend this to you, Gentlemen, as the first and best way of discipline: since by setting down exactly what you think about a book or a poem, you not only clarify your view (and are concurrently learning to write or talk with precision), but your mistakes are the more easily corrected by others or by yourself, and so (as Robert Bridges puts it in his Essay on Keats) the true business of criticism is advanced. Nay, if you incline to despise it as a creeping method in comparison with the practice of high-sounding generalities, remind yourselves that this was Aristotle's way, who examined the stuff the Poets wrote with a naturalist's eye and was content to build his inductions upon that, giving his reasons. Also, and notably, it was Samuel Johnson's way. Coming (say) upon a couple of lines in *The Merchant of Venice*, Act v, where Stephano, Portia's butler, announces her return by daybreak to Belmont—'Who comes with her?' demands Lorenzo, and is answered

>None but a holy hermit and her maid.

—Johnson succinctly observed, 'I do not perceive the use of this hermit'—and lo! upon search, nor does anyone else. Again, after wrestling with an obscure or corrupt passage, he is apt to confess 'I can make nothing of this': and that is why one returns always to Johnson's track on any puzzling passage in Shakespeare. He may be right or wrong: but an acute and honest mind has been before you. You always know where you are with him. Or, if you will, open at any chance page of the *Lives of the Poets*. At this point at a venture I myself opened the book on his 'Life of Pope', and on the page where he compares Pope's *Ode for Saint Cecilia's Day* with Dryden's, which it obviously challenged. Stanza by stanza he examines it, line almost by line. Again, it was a habit with Lamb and Hazlitt, in their dealings with the older dramatists, to print selected passages alongside their comments, that the reader might at any point test the justice of these by instant reference to the author's actual words, and I think that Matthew Arnold showed a like instinct for definiteness, albeit in a different way, when he exhibited (as you remember) particular lines of Homer, Dante, Chaucer, Shakespeare, Pope, Burns, as touchstones of poetic seriousness in varying degrees. You may hold with me that he chose some of his exhibits with caprice, or take offence at something school-masterish in his method. He could not help *that*; being, all his days and congenitally as well as professionally, addicted to Education.

This view which I am trying to persuade you to accept with me—of the prime value of definiteness in criticising—of playing, so to speak, 'on the ball'— should not be despised for being elementary. It is told of Nelson that when he assembled his Captains and explained to them beforehand the plan of action by which he proposed to win at Trafalgar, many of them wept—so daring and beautiful it seemed to them in conception: but that he added 'In any doubt or confusion of battle no Captain is likely to go far wrong who claps his ship aboard one of the enemy'. And of Coleridge in especial this view involves the regret that Coleridge, who can play 'on the ball' so brilliantly, so often drops it and wanders off: a defeat on which I may quote Mr T. S. Eliot—

Coleridge's metaphysical interest was quite genuine, and was, like most metaphysical interest, an affair of the emotions. But

ON BEING DEFINITE

a literary critic should have no emotions except those immediately provoked by a work of art.... Coleridge is apt to take leave of the data of criticism, and arouse the suspicion that he has been diverted by a metaphysical hare-and-hounds. His end does not always appear to be the return to the work of art with improved perception and intensified, because more conscious, enjoyment; his centre of interest changes.... In the derogatory sense he is more 'philosophic' than Aristotle. For everything that Aristotle says illuminates the literature which is the occasion for saying it; but Coleridge only now and then.

III

Further, it is well worth our while to note how entertaining and instructive these metaphysicians can be when they put off their beards and discuss actual material with which the poets provide them, and contrast this with the vacuity in which they lose themselves when they resume these solemn appendages and legislate on generalities. I pass by the natural human distrust of pontifical talk, the natural human demand for persuasion as the only intellectual process to which a free man should surrender. Their graver mistake lies in the assumption that they can *comprehend* what the poets but *apprehend*, and can mete out poetry as gods; whereas none but a God can comprehend. Else Jack were not only as good as his Master but demonstrably better, being able to comprehend God. That seems to me the last reason why Wordsworth, being a poet, in practice makes his own theories look silly: and that, I take it, is what Mr Richards means (it has of course struck others but he observes it appositely and I name him as Cicero would say 'for the sake of honour') when he accuses

Dr Bradby at one point of 'talking about Poetry and the *poetic* instead of thinking about the concrete experiences, which are poems' and adds that 'his is the concrete and not unfamiliar case of a critic whose practice is a refutation of his principles'.

Let us take, for example, the admired Signor Croce. He deals with Ariosto, and after telling us in a footnote (for so eminent a scholar, gratuitously) that he has examined all, or almost all, the literature of erudition and criticism in connection with Ariosto, he writes on Ariosto an essay which is a little classic in itself: and again on Shakespeare (though here he cannot, as no man can, claim acquaintance with all that erudition and criticism has piled upon Shakespeare—God forbid!), he writes with liveliness and understanding of the man and his work and is, in the best sense, amusing; whereas in his Aesthetic and other portentous writings without reference to such practitioners as Ariosto or Shakespeare, he works out that Alpha = Beta, which again = Gamma, and so on to Omega, which, equalling Alpha, dismisses us by the same door wherein we went. That the first business of criticising a creative author is to enter, so far as possible, into his mind everybody knows and always has known: that by any such process however criticism makes itself one with creative poetic power, everyone knows to be an error who knows the difference between making a boot and knowing where it pinches. Nor is there any question of comparative dignity: one man makes a boot, another wears it, and there is the original relation between art and criticism.

The power of mere theoric to revive itself a score of

times after defeat, reclothe itself in tradition, and browbeat common sense by dogma, daunts the timidly receptive mind or even converts it to the rage of the sheep. Even so level-headed a writer as the late Professor Spingarn, for example, is caught up into such an ecstasy by the whirlwind of Croce that almost he exclaims with Elisha, 'My father! the chariots of Israel and the horsemen thereof!' Once get it into your head (he assures us) that all art is just a form of expression, and you get rid of almost everything that has hitherto passed for Criticism. It is all so much lumber, and he lists it—

(*a*) We have done (he says) with all the old Rules. Yes: though one had supposed them done with, and done for, long ago.

(*b*) We have done with all literary *kinds*—tragedy, comedy, epic, lyric, pastoral. One had supposed with Aristotle that in epic the poet told the story in his own person, in tragedy by actors saying and doing things on a stage. But no: 'there are not three or ten or any limited number of literary kinds: there are as many kinds as there are individual poets'.

(*c*) We have done with the theory of style:—as presumably we should in daily life do without regiment of manners; each of us, for example, using his knife and fork as instruments of self-expression.

(*d*) 'We have done with all moral judgment of literature'—'all', mark you! 'If the ideals enunciated by poets are not those we admire most, we must blame not the poets but ourselves: in the world where morals count we have failed to give them the proper material out of which to rear a nobler edifice.' So, if the ideals enunciated by Hollywood are not those you admire most, the fault, dear Brutus, lies not with the 'Stars' but in yourself, for having neglected to provide them with material for a nobler edifice. To be sure an accident in time has prevented your providing (say) Peter of Aretino with material for edification, and so—

(*e*) Out goes the history and criticism of poetic themes.... We have done with the race, the time, the environment of a poet's work.

A Sumnour was there with us in that place...

Who, reading Chaucer's *Prologue* in so easy a vacuum, wants to know what a Sumnour was, or a Franklyn or a Pardoner, or what were their various businesses in life? Out these pilgrims go, with (for I have not exhausted the list) technique, emotion, any distinction between genius and taste, or distinct notion even of what Chaucer, for example, is talking about. In short we have emptied out the baby with the bath-water; or, to vary the metaphor (but Dr Spingarn has no use for metaphor), with each successive jettison of ballast our balloon recedes higher and higher from earth into an empyrean where the temporary caprice of a chosen people reasserts itself as King's Writ.—'In those days there were no Judges in Israel: every man did that which was right in his own eyes.'

But even a less excitable disciple than Professor Spingarn will sometimes betray giddiness when he leans across the golden bar (so to speak) and looks down upon those fretful midges, the poets. Take for example the late Dr Wildon Carr, a learned man and an Aristotelian to boot. Glancing at a light shaft which Croce has levelled at Ruskin, Dr Carr explains to us that

> Ruskin may well stand as the type of a class of writers on aesthetic of whom many and famous examples belong to our own country and literature. They are artists who criticise art. They are deeply versed in the philosophy of art and often give us profound insight into it, but their main direction is not towards a philosophy of art indifferent to any particular production; it is towards art itself and its appreciation. We go to them, for example, to enhance our enjoyment of the work of Polycleitus or Michelangelo, of Dante or of Beethoven. We do not go to them as we go to Kant or to Schopenhauer or to Schelling or to Hegel, *whose aesthetic appreciation may be no whit above the vulgar*, for a theory of art itself.

Now without enquiring why we should go for any theories of art to men who—their aesthetic appreciation being no whit above the vulgar—by hypothesis lack capacity to separate wrong from right, good from less good, less good from utterly bad, in the subject on which they talk, we may agree that for our present purpose, for criticism of 'the stuff the poets have written' we do not go to Schelling or Hegel. We go—to whom? Surely we go to Ben Jonson, or to Sidney, or to Milton, or to Dryden, or to Pope, or to Addison, or to Samuel Johnson, or to Coleridge, or to Blake, or to Charles Lamb, or to Matthew Arnold, or to Patmore, or to Mr T. S. Eliot; that is, to men who have either written noble numbers, or have at least practised the art with some success. Mr Eliot tells us that the reason why the artist is—each within his own limitations—oftenest to be depended upon as a critic consists in the likelihood that 'his criticism will be criticism, and not the satisfaction of a suppressed creative wish—which, in most other persons is apt to interfere fatally'. I might put it more bluntly. We go to him because he has been at pains to practise before he preaches.

IV

In a recent and gallant attempt to include *An Outline of Modern Knowledge* within the covers of one volume the editor and publisher were fortunate enough to enlist Professor Lascelles Abercrombie to provide the section on 'Principles of Literary Criticism', and in his contribution the professor maintains, despite of Croce, that 'the realm of literature is occupied by the activities of three distinct powers; the power to create, the power to enjoy, and the power to criticise'; and this may do well enough for us if we observe the warning that while these three powers are distinct, and of the three the chief thing that distinguishes the power to criticise from the other two is the fact that it can be acquired, yet the three are interdependent; for obviously a main purpose of creating poetry is to produce something enjoyable, and as obviously one of the main purposes of criticism is to improve enjoyment by cultivating in us what Dr Johnson would call an 'increased sensibility'.

V

In concluding this lecture I venture to offer an example, quite elementary, to illustrate my contention that by examining a poem definitely, and examining it with patience, we may make it yield an enjoyment which carelessness has overlooked.

I will take Hood's *Ode to Autumn*; so often compared, to its detriment, with the more exquisite one by Keats. Undoubtedly it echoes Keats' ode (Hood, as you know, had steeped himself in admiration of Keats). Where Keats, speaking of Autumn and its 'mellow fruitfulness', asks

> Where are the songs of Spring? Ay, where are they?

Hood, whose autumn is rather the November of bare branches and whistling winds, asks

> Where are the blooms of Summer?

and his conclusion

> Enough of fear and shadowy despair,
> To frame her cloudy prison for the soul!

obviously recalls the conclusion of Keats' *Ode to Melancholy*

> His soul shall taste the sadness of her might,
> And be among her cloudy trophies hung.

But if I confess here a particular affection for Hood's poem, it is not the affection of one

> Singularly moved
> To love the lovely that is least beloved.

My purpose is rather to vindicate it from an accusation brought (so far as I know) by every previous critic. But first let me read you the poem.

ODE

AUTUMN

I saw old Autumn in the misty morn
Stand shadowless like Silence, listening
To silence, for no lonely bird would sing
Into his hollow ear from woods forlorn,
Nor lowly hedge nor solitary thorn;
Shaking his languid locks all dewy bright
With tangled gossamer that fell by night,
    Pearling his coronet of golden corn.

Where are the songs of Summer?—With the sun,
Oping the dusky eyelids of the south,
Till shade and silence waken up as one,
And Morning sings with a warm odorous mouth.
Where are the merry birds?—Away, away,
On panting wings through the inclement skies,
    Lest owls should prey
    Undazzled at noon-day,
And tear with horny beak their lustrous eyes.

Where are the blooms of Summer?—In the west,
Blushing their last to the last sunny hours,
When the mild Eve by sudden Night is prest
Like tearful Proserpine, snatch'd from her flow'rs
    To a most gloomy breast.

Where is the pride of Summer,—the green prime,—
The many, many leaves all twinkling?—Three
On the moss'd elm; three on the naked lime
Trembling,—and one upon the old oak tree!
    Where is the Dryad's immortality?—
Gone into mournful cypress and dark yew,
Or wearing the long gloomy Winter through
    In the smooth holly's green eternity.

ON BEING DEFINITE

The squirrel gloats on his accomplish'd hoard,
The ants have brimm'd their garners with ripe grain,
    And honey bees have stored
The sweets of summer in their luscious cells;
The swallows all have wing'd across the main;
And here the Autumn melancholy dwells,
    And sighs her tearful spells

Amongst the sunless shadows of the plain.
    Alone, alone,
    Upon a mossy stone,
She sits and reckons up the dead and gone,
With the last leaves for a love-rosary;
Whilst all the wither'd world looks drearily,
Like a dim picture of the drowned past
In the hush'd mind's mysterious far-away,
Doubtful what ghostly thing will steal the last
Into that distance, grey upon the grey.

O go and sit with her, and be o'ershaded
Under the languid downfall of her hair;
She wears a coronal of flowers faded
Upon her forehead, and a face of care;—
There is enough of sadness to invite,
If only for the rose that died, whose doom
Is Beauty's,—she that with the living bloom
Of conscious cheeks most beautifies the light:
There is enough of sorrowing, and quite
Enough of bitter fruits the earth doth bear,—
Enough of chilly droppings from her bowl;
Enough of fear and shadowy despair,
To frame her cloudy prison for the soul!

  The common accusation brought against Hood is that he here makes of Autumn two confused persons, a male and a female. But one minute alteration, not even of a word but of a letter will convince you, I think, that he does nothing of the sort. For 'Autumn melancholy' read 'autumn Melancholy' with the capitals transposed (as I guess they were by the printer), and you perceive that in the first part of his ode he is presenting Autumn in the figure of a man, in the second he turns to Autumn's spouse, bride, leman, what you will—to Autumn's inseparable companion, that gentle melancholy which must ever accompany our thoughts with the fall of the year, faithful to her man as Sorrow in Keats' *Song of the Indian Maid*

> To Sorrow
> I bade good morrow,
> And thought to leave her far away behind;
> But cheerly, cheerly,
> She loves me dearly;
> She is so constant to me, and so kind:
> I would deceive her,
> And so leave her,
> But ah! she is so constant and so kind....
>
> There is not one,
> No, no, not one
> But thee to comfort a poor lonely maid;
> Thou art her mother,
> And her brother,
> Her playmate, and her wooer in the shade.

In other words, from an objective presentation of Autumn, with which Keats contented himself, Hood turns to that subjective, more feminine, side and weds the union in our minds.

You may or may not agree with my own conclusion in this quite elementary instance—but at least you will see the method—of learning to practise your criticism

ON BEING DEFINITE

of poetry upon the poetry itself before you start upon prying into the poet's private life. Poetry is an achievement by a poet *in his best moments*. No true poet ever wrote a poem as a proposed exposition of his own personality. Then why will critics, as the fashion now is, persist in treating his work as *that*—as its τὸ τί ἦν εἶναι, its 'what it was meant to be'?—on this assumption themselves 'assuming the god' and explaining a man's best by hunting out his private lapses or frailties? Of such critics I would demand, as Isabella demanded of Angelo—

>How would *you* be,
>If He, which is the top of judgement, should
>But judge *you* as you are?

FIRST AID IN CRITICISING. II

A NOTE ON THE *POETICS*

I

THE *Poetics* of Aristotle can scarcely be called a treatise, or even—fragment though it is—the fragment of a revised treatise. Nevertheless, and as it stands, it has for the student of literary criticism a double historical value apart from its own inherent merit. It is the first examination known to us of the poetical art, and ever since its re-discovery it has exercised an amazing pollency upon all critical minds, throughout Europe. It has been used as Bible and misinterpreted as Bible; and its misinterpretations have, translated into laws and practice, commanded a century and more of dramatic literature. It has been slavishly obeyed, violently controverted. The historical fact remains that all critical writers have to reckon their start with it. In short it is Elementary.

Being Elementary, it is (in my experience) the very best start for a learner. But being also seminal, it suggests thoughts which, between teacher and pupil, can be carried into many paths, as well as used for friendly correction of judgment. It has that final majesty which resides in ministry, the innocent cunning to be universal while practical. It is upon some few of its quite elementary points that I invite your attention to-day.

II

Let us start with a very few words on its shape, scope and intention. It is (as I have said) a fragment. Laying itself out to discuss the poetic art in general, it passes on to deal with Tragedy, discusses this carefully, compares it to its advantage with Epic, and then suddenly breaks off. Everyone to-day allows that a Second Part, dealing with the Epic itself, with Comedy, if not also with the Lyric or Dithyramb, was intended, and possibly followed. But that Second Part has been lost.

Further, the *reliquiae*, as they have come down to us, while mostly pure Aristotle in style as in matter, are in later parts—here and there—careless, shorthand, or idly repetitive passages, which suggest that we owe what we have to no revision by the Master, but to notes by a pupil who in time yielded to that end-of-term feeling we all know so well, and was occasionally the victim of an abrupt question, thrown at him to wake him up.

As for its early fame. There is no evidence at all (or none known to me) that the Alexandrine critics, or their Roman successors in Rhetoric, esteemed it of palmary, even of considerable, importance—that is, if we cut out Horace's unacknowledged borrowings for the *Ars Poetica*. It must have impressed more oriental races somehow, for it survived in Arabic and Syriac translation: but for medieval Europe, it was, until the second half of the fifteenth century, a lost book. Even when, in the thirteenth century, the drive out of Byzantium opened up its libraries to the West and *the*

Philosopher started to resume that sway over the intelligence of Europe which he has, ever since, maintained and improved, his *Rhetoric* found a translator as a matter of course, but our little treatise was 'left out in the cold', even outside the doors of the great Aldine Aristotle of 1495–8.

It does not fall within the scope of my purpose to-day, Gentlemen, to rehearse the story of this Cinderella. One could easily embroider it with many historical ornaments—as, for a single instance, with the story of the first real commentator—Castelvetro—one of those diabolical crossword-puzzle men, camp-followers in the commissariat of any humanistic movement since time began—who, with his numerous brothers and their wives, held supper-parties at Modena, highbrow gatherings at which every guest had to compose a Greek or a Latin epigram, or at least an Italian sonnet or a madrigal, and all had to discourse in the language selected by the President of the Feast for that evening. Picture these feasts. I instance Castelvetro—*pedantuccio e grammataccio* as a testy contemporary called him—only because, as about the earliest to squeeze a foot into the glass slipper, he exhibited the resultant corns as Rules, imposed them as such upon the great French tragedians of the seventeenth century, and had to be exposed in England by the common sense of Dryden, later by Samuel Johnson, until it remained only for my predecessor in this Chair to enquire, with a beautiful simplicity, 'How did this nonsense ever come to be talked by men of sense?'

But Castelvetro's and other men's vagaries are but

parentheses in the statement of an undeniable fact—that from the moment this little, unshapely book was re-born into our Western world it has simply taken charge of all the art of Criticising, constraining all critics. They may contradict, confute, cut themselves with knives: they may misinterpret with Castelvetro, partly interpret with Milton or Lessing, misunderstand with Edgar Allen Poe and George Henry Lewes, curse with Dallas, patronise with Croce. But not one of them can disregard or get away from it.

III

And why?

Well, for three good reasons: of which the first is the most trivial. It happens to be, so far as is known, the earliest attempt to treat Poetry as a branch of man's Natural History. Even for this it has more than an antiquarian interest; being an actual datum for any study on man's development as a thinking animal. As Newman put it in a slightly different connection, 'In a language's earlier times, while it is yet unformed, to write in it at all is almost a work of genius. It is like crossing a country before roads are made communicating between place and place. The authors of that age deserve to be Classics, both because of what they do and because they can do it'. Newman was speaking in particular of pioneers in pure *literature*, early framers of a nation's verse or prose. But his words apply just as well to those who break the ground and draw the first furrow in any field of human thought.

Our business to-day, however, does not lie with this historical precedence of the *Poetics*. I but remind you of it, and pass on to some points which more nearly concern us as learners in the Art of Criticising.

IV

For the first, there is that virtue of his method which I commended to you in my preceding lecture—the simple, direct way of taking poetry as the actual 'stuff the poets wrote' and 'getting on to *that*' as a naturalist would: a thing to be wondered at, no doubt as a spider's web might be wondered at, or the convolutions of a sea-shell, or the starry pattern of a crystal; but first of all to be observed, noted, with a curiosity in the thing for its own sake; also, no doubt, in the permanent hope of all men of science, that by accumulating observed facts and divining their right arrangement some general conclusions may be drawn—with this difference, of course, that Poetry, the object examined, being a *human* faculty or activity, these conclusions may be of use to future men, as no observations by a naturalist can as yet (so far as we know) instruct the future spider or mollusc to rise on stepping-stones of his dead self to higher things. I speak cautiously here; since there is no telling what the Mendelians may or may not do some day—and an oyster may then be eugenically crossed in love. And I speak, of course, under Aristotle's own insistent reservation that no study of man's doings—be it in politics, ethics, any form of his industry or art or worldly activity—can be conducted on any line of mathematical demonstration: the whole business must depend on induction, a process so complicated by individual freaks of reason or passion that whereas Poetry, for instance, can persuade you convincingly of what, in given circumstances, Alcibiades would have done and suffered, History at any moment may produce evidence that he did precisely the opposite, and escaped the fatal consequences.

But, this granted, who can help admiring the way Aristotle goes to work? He is always, as I put it last time, 'on the ball', and that ball, Epic or Tragedy, always close to his toe. You may dissent from this or that opinion of his on this play or that passage in it. But there it is: you know just where you are, and why. You may hold, for instance (as I humbly do), that his insistence on *Plot* in a drama tempts him to over-estimate his pet *Oedipus* ('Cover his face'), to ignore the calm cruelty of so much in its 'perfect' author. But there you have his preference and his reason for it, chapter and verse.

And that is why, though he could only deal with the poetry existing in his day, his book remains the norm of the art in which we are learners. I dare not prophesy that it always will so remain: but will rather imitate the caution which he used in speaking of the development of Tragedy.—

If it be asked whether Tragedy has yet arrived at being all that it need be in form—to decide that theoretically in relation to the Theatre is another question—all we can say is that its advance was by little and little, as the poets discovered improvements, until it reached its natural metre, and there stopped.

Not even an Aristotle could foretell a Shakespeare, or deal with that which Time took almost two thousand years in bringing to birth. Nevertheless, by working on the evidence he had, and working on the method of examining definite concrete works, he derived conclusions by which we can test Shakespeare himself again and again, always with profit and no small wonder. For an example, if you take his reasoned definition of the Tragic Hero, as

a man of high prosperity, good but not eminently good nor just, whose misfortune is brought about by no vice or depravity, but through some error (ἁμαρτία) or frailty...

and apply this successively to Macbeth, Coriolanus, Brutus, Hamlet, Othello, Lear, Antony (all great, all even noble, all so different in their ways), and you will hardly withhold your wonder at the man or—my immediate point—your respectful admiration of his method.

V

Next, I will ask you to consider how, throughout the little treatise—sometimes explicitly, but ever as a thing understood—Aristotle handles Poetry as no mere ornament but a natural function of man, to create or enjoy, and, as a beautiful function, therefore a natural grace of life. It is no 'Criticism of Life', save and in so far as all Art is that. I suppose there are few now but would condemn Matthew Arnold's as an ill-fitting definition, at once too loose and too strait—while none the more ingratiating by that smatch of the Schoolmaster which unregenerate man so properly abhors. Nor on the other hand shall I who spent some of my youth in combating 'Art for Art's Sake' waste any fraction of your youth, or of my own declining years, in discussing that other extreme of doctrine. We are talking of Aristotle, who—understanding most things—would scarcely have understood what 'Art for Art's Sake' meant. Indeed I have always regretted that Butcher's most useful edition of the *Poetics* should be labelled *Aristotle's Theory of Poetry and Fine Art*. It misleads. To Aristotle *any* art—that of Poetry included—would be a fine art just in proportion as it was fine; as carpentry, for instance, or pottery, would be a fine art if finely practised. One art could, and did, serve another—as, let us say, statuary serves architecture. But as for separating the arts by invidious category, into arts fine in themselves, and arts not fine in themselves, Aristotle had no idea of it. Indeed I am ready to assert that nowhere in his published works can you find a term translatable as 'Fine Art'; and I am reasonably certain that had he felt any need for any such term, he had the capacity to invent one.

No the arts—all of them—to him, as to any other Greek—were just parts in the education of a gentleman: that is to say, of a perfect citizen.

You may get at this—to take an example most pertinent to us—by considering his famous definition of the use of Tragedy as 'through Pity and Terror purging these emotions in us'. The word Katharsis or 'purge'—'pill' if you like—is now generally, and after much delicate paraphrasing in more squeamish times, recognised for what it is—a straight medical word used by a naturalist to convey that Tragedy operates on the mind, to cleanse it, as certain laxatives will do on the body. (And Apollo, let me again remind you, was father alike of Song and of Medicine.) That is all: and almost all the fuss about it just clears itself away when you compare this supposedly difficult passage with others in other works of the Master. Then you will perceive that the purpose of all the separate arts is to cleanse a man of his 'humours' and recall his system to the normal. Tragedy, by its dose of pity and terror, showing him overweening pride, ambition, lust, exaggerated in a spectacle of kings and princes, will teach him to discharge these accretions of self-pity, self-esteem, vaulting ambition, tyrannical pride, unreasonable terrors from his soul, and dismiss him with

> calm of mind, all passion spent.

But even such an operation—if you will look into the *Politics*—does Music. Music, by its regulated beat, effects a Katharsis of 'enthusiasm'. Music, if I may use the illustration, corrects the sort of vocality to which unbridled man gives way in his bath. Rhetoric similarly (if rightly employed) corrects to genuine persuasiveness the tendency on the one hand to gush, on the other to legal hairsplitting and making the worse argument seem the better. Comedy canalises the right man's mirth between laughter at things not properly ridiculous and the mere hysterical *fou rire*. Even dancing regulates, by rhythm, the less moderate tendencies of the human leg.

All these, in short, coalesce into one system of the arts—that of using for good man's emotions regulated and controlled by reason: all together moulding him back to that temperance, that σωφροσύνη which results in a cultivated man who is also an exemplary citizen.

VI

Let us turn, now, to a more particular lesson of the *Poetics*. Aristotle starts off by telling us that 'Epic Poetry and Tragedy, Comedy, Lyric, even flute-playing and lyre-playing are all, speaking generally, modes of *Imitation*'. The word *Mimesis*, translated literally as 'Imitation' of course, is just as defensibly accurate as the late Mr Paley's habitual rapturous rendering of γυναῖκες in a Greek chorus by 'the female population'.

That, of course, is the trouble with all our efforts to convey any word from one language to another with its exact meaning or its shades of meaning. As Professor Ker (*valde deflendus*) complained ten years since—

> In the other Arts there is nothing like the curse of Babel: but the divine Idea of Poetry, abiding the same with itself in essence, shining with the same light, as Drummond sees it in Homer and Virgil, Ronsard and Garcillasso de la Vega, is actually seen by very few votaries in each and all of these several lamps. The light of Poetry may be all over the world and belong to the whole human race, yet how little of it is really available, compared with the other arts! It is broken up among the various languages....

In a previous lecture I have asked you to accept 'Representation' as the nearest word in English for Aristotle's 'Mimesis'. It does not, it cannot, as I have tried to show, preclude originality or personality, however modest of himself an author may be. So *he* be true, a pattern will push up through his weaving. As my late friend Sir Walter Raleigh has put it, speaking of Shakespeare, 'No man can walk save in his own shadow', and an author friend, Sir Henry Newbolt, in an epistle dedicatory to one of his books—

I have heard [he says] of certain mirrors made in the far East which show not only a reflection of the scene before them but a picture of their own as well, a constant and inseparable pattern appearing from beneath their visible surface and interweaving itself with every representation of the outer world. Surely the mind of man is such a mirror, and that which he writes just such a constant and inevitable transformation of that which he has seen.

VII

Having started on this question of *Mimesis*, or Representation, I shall ask you to consider, next time, some of the handicaps and limitations of writing, and also some of its natural advantages in comparison with certain sister arts—Painting, Statuary, Music: what it is almost constrained to do less well than these, what it can do inestimably better, and even (I fear) how some of its proper handicaps have been now and again expertly dodged: and this for the practical purpose of deciding where any given passage of Literature is doing its own proper business, or with what success attempting another's.

But to-day we will have no quarrel with the sister Muses, confining ourselves, for a crucial test, to one particular thing which Literature (which is memorable speech), and only Literature, can attempt; which almost defies success, and yet must be attempted for man's edification, if poet, priest or prophet wish to convey to him any convinced message concerning his place in this Universe, or his relation to the Will that created and directs it.

I mean *articulate speech by a Deity*.

VIII

To the Greeks this would present no very great difficulty, their gods being numerous, friendly, very like men in passion, differing little from men indeed save for their immortality and an aura of beauty, a lustre, which in their goings and comings they could summon all artifices to conceal. Phoebus Apollo, for example, could be sentenced to serve the flocks of Admetus: or, set free, could ask his way of any shepherd of the hills and challenge him to pipe a duet. And among the audience of a poet reporting such an incident there might be many who seriously claimed to derive their own progeniture as an accident of some such visitation among the daughters and sons of earth. Even Zeus held his throne on no secure tenure, and had frequently, after thundering, to justify himself. Aristotle, to be sure, deprecates any intrusion of the God into a drama in which mortals 'do things': Gods should be restricted to the Prologue: and I think we may admit that the intrusion of Herakles—a demi-god only—into the *Alcestis* left Aristotle with the last word on this point.

But when we come to the Hebrews and to the conception of one Deity, uncreate, invisible, incomprehensible, eternal, how are you to do it in language—which nevertheless is the divinest gift of man, separating him from the brutes? How are we (if I may use a vulgar term with reverence) to 'make conversation'?

Well, the idea of the Israelites—that they were a chosen folk, selected to cherish this idea of an Invisible Father while they ousted mere materialistic and idolatrous tribes—was helped, of course, enormously by the anthropomorphic sense of Him as a particular Father, a jealous Father, well aware of His *patria potestas*, not unwilling to chide and use the rod; conveying his precepts in language understandable by man. Else how could man obey?

Even so, this nation had found out a way—that of stark-naked simplicity. '*I am that I Am*' or 'Thou shalt say to the children of Israel, *I Am* hath sent me unto you'—there is no rhetoric or argument about that! And, even so, in a strange but famous passage Longinus—noting that the pagan way of allowing the deities to squabble, be jealous in amours, be wounded and scream in battle, if not impious, yet violates our sense of what is fitting—continues,

> Thus [Moses] the legislator of the Jews, no ordinary man, having framed and declared a worthy conception of the Godhead, writes in the very beginning of his Laws, 'God said—What? "Let there be Light", and there was Light: "let there be Land", and there was Land'.

When we come to the Prophets in our Bible or even to the Book of Job (which is, of course, a different matter) we find men who magnificently embroider this simplicity and make God speak gloriously (as in their turn our English translators attest).

Hast thou an arm like God?... Dost thou know the balancing of the clouds?... Canst thou bind the sweet influences of Pleiades or loose the bands of Orion?

or again—

And he said unto me, 'In the beginning, when the earth was made, before the borders of the world stood, or ever the winds blew.... Before the fair flowers were seen, or ever the moveable powers were established, before the innumerable multitude of angels were gathered together.... Or ever the chimneys in Sion were hot, and or ever the inventions of them that now sin were turned, before they were sealed that have gathered faith for a treasure: then did I consider these things, and they all were made through me alone, and through none other: by me also shall they be ended, and by none other'.

The magnitude of such language I have preached from this desk before now. But one or two reflections occur for our warning. The first is the assumed nearness of Jehovah to these men, and His immediate inspiration. He had laid a coal of fire on their lips, or they had swallowed a roll of His word which they reproduced instrumentally. The second must dwell in that fallacy of the anthropomorphic, which no man—and these prophets, perhaps, least of all—could escape: the fallacy of making an Almighty *argue*—the essence of any argument being that it, at least, invites an answer. That is—always must be—the trouble with making Omnipotence speak rhetorically.

Turn from the Hebrews to Milton and you find the Almighty made to speak majestically indeed, but at a scholastic remove: in that diapason which Milton above any of our poets could command, but in a literary thunder with the *vox humana*—of man's friend—here missing as a stop, here, where pulled out, somehow intrusive—I will not say querulous—but certainly argumentative. Take, for example, the sonorous approval of Christ in the Third Book, and watch how with its 'because', and 'because' and 'therefore' it weakens from authority to justification: which hardly beseems the speaker or His angelic audience, who for poetic purposes had done better some years before 'in burning row' with their 'loud uplifted trumpets'. Here indeed is the basic flaw of our great Epic: to start Omniscience arguing is as superfluous as challenging Omnipotence to fight. Satan in the story has no call to explain himself. His cause is prejudged, his defeat determined. But he faces up to it with our sympathy. In short Milton's God, creating man in His image, forgot to anticipate his development into a sportsman. Yet why do I dally with this, when a friend has done it for me so much better than I have either time or power to do? Read Mr Tillyard's study of Milton.

But it is when we come to the eighteenth century in England, to poets who successively in an Age of Reason tried to make the Deity talk like John Milton, that this anthropomorphic fallacy of putting rhetoric into the mouth of Jehovah crumbles away gradually, as stucco off a fishing-house of the period. It lasted on until the year 1827, anyhow.

No one of you who has haunted a second-hand bookstall can have failed to take up, it may be often, a certain epic of that date. It is almost always bound in full calf

A NOTE ON THE *POETICS*

or morocco, tooled and gilt: within the cover you will commonly find an inscription in italic hand by a lady to a gentleman who has, through marriage, missed his way. The inscription does not say this in so many words: but I have noted that the recipient seems always to have married, already or subsequently, some other than the donor. The price ranges around one-and-sixpence: the date may be anything after 1827, and the title is Pollok's *Course of Time*.

It ends with a terrific description of the Day of Judgment: and my own very handsome copy of it, inherited from a Grandfather (who, by the way, did not marry the donor—it was a fatal gift!), bears the date 1829. And this is how Robert Pollok, Master of Arts, makes God speak—

> Long have I stood, as ye, my sons, well know,
> Between the cherubim. . . .
> Have I not early risen, and sent my seers,
> Prophets, apostles, teachers, ministers,
> With signs and wonders working in my name?
> Have I not still from age to age raised up
> As I saw needful great religious men?

And so, these questions being unanswerable by the Assembly, the sword of Justice is drawn, in hand omnipotent,

> And down among the damned the burning edge
> Plunged. . . .

Now I do not wish to make a mock of any man doing his best (and Pollok died young) even though my own boyhood suffered tortured nights from a great deal of that kind of thing. But I will just ask you to oppose to it for literary sincerity (and, I would add, human decency) the simple fashion in which some of our medieval fathers, when they made God talk at all, tried to convey Him. We have been considering—let me remind you—the problem of Representation. My first example is the opening of *Everyman*. *Deus loquitur*—

> I perceive here in my majesty
> How that all creatures be to me unkind,
> Living without dread in worldly prosperity.
> Of ghostly sight the people be so blind,
> Drowned in sin, they know me not for their God;
> In worldly riches is all their mind.
> They fear not my righteousness, that sharp rod;
>   My law that I showed, when I for them died,
> They forget clean, and shedding of my blood so red.
> I hanged between two thieves, it cannot be denied,
> To get them life, I suffered to be dead;
> I healed their feet—with thorns hurt was my head—
> I could do no more than I did, truly.
> And now I see the people do clean forsake me;
> They use the seven deadly sins damnable;
> As pride, covetise, wrath, and lechery,
> Now in the world be made commendable;
> And thus they leave of angels the heavenly company.

Next, hear Christ speaking in his complaint as a Lover of Man's soul—*Quia Amore Langueo*:

> I crowned her with bliss and she me with thorn;
> I led her to chamber and she me to die;
> I brought her to worship and she me to scorn;
> I did her reverence and she me villany.
> To love that loveth is no maistry;
> Her hate made never my love her foe;
> Ask me then no question why—
>   Quia amore langueo.

We cannot, in these days, make Divinity speak just so. It is a loss we have suffered through doubt and sophistication. That sweet and sincere simplicity we can no more recover to-day than the delightful ignorance of a primitive painter. To attempt it is to sophisticate backward upon our own sophistication. Therein lies the trap of present-day medievalism. What we have to do in our own day, aware of a vast surrounding ignorance, is to be honest in dealing with the little that man has won from it.

FIRST AID IN CRITICISING. III

THE HANDICAP OF POETRY

I

IN my last lecture, Gentlemen, we agreed—or, to speak more precisely, I asked you to agree—that 'Representation' is as fair and close-fitting a word as we can find in English for that *Mimesis* of which Aristotle asserts Poetry and Music, in their various kinds, to be alike modes in their way. But if 'Representation' cover the invisible art of Music even more obviously it covers the plastic arts of Painting, Sculpture, Architecture. The painter represents a figure or a landscape for us, or a group of what is termed 'still life': and Aristotle even supposed us to delight in the resemblance of a portrait to the original, exclaiming 'This is he!' If with some more modern critics we prefer to exclaim delightedly 'This is not in the least like him!' still our 'reaction'—to use their favourite word—is to the same presentment immediate. The sculptor adds a dimension, and represents the forms of men, of beasts, even of gods as he conceives them and wishes us to recognise them: the architect again draws a structure for men's defence, habitation, or occasional worship. Here we may be disappointed by the building when we come to live in it: but his first art is to represent a building and persuade us at first sight that it *is* a building and designed for a particular purpose. 'Hulloa!', said Mr Wemmick on a famous occasion, 'Here's a Church! Let's get married'.

II

Now the differences among the arts; the limitations imposed upon this one and that by their proper material, or the dimensions in which they work, whether of time or space; their allowable licence to steal from another's province; all these questions have engaged philosophical critics from Lessing down and even before Lessing. For our elementary purpose I propose to indicate to-day only a few salient differences, as guides to determining of a given passage in any writer—

First, if he be doing that which *his* art can do and no other, or can do better than another; and

Secondly if he be of hardihood or necessity raiding another's province; and, if so, with what success? [We will not say 'with what justification?' For we are presumably young as judges, and we shall soon be dealing with genius; and genius has ever claimed to go back to

—the good old rule, the simple plan
That they may take who have the power
And they may keep who can.]

III

Let us, then, starting with the obvious, select to consider the rivalries of Painting and Poetry.

The old legend says that Zeuxis painted a cluster of grapes so life-like that the birds tried to peck at it:

whereupon his rival Parrhasius set a canvas in front painted so like a curtain that Zeuxis tried to draw it. Well, we can all see that curtain for ourselves nowadays, on the proscenium of many a theatre; if Greek painting had not risen above *that* (and it has perished, but we have Aristotle's assurance elsewhere that it *did*, Polygnotus 'painting men better than they are') why, then, it would have achieved but the narrowest kind of *Mimesis*, a trickwork of imitation, of mere copying. But the little game between Zeuxis and Parrhasius may illustrate our argument, which here concerns but the means, the material, and the process.

A painter desires to paint, let us say, a tree—a tree in its summer leafage. If it be set in a landscape he will treat it in less detail than if it be a representation of one particular tree: and even in detail he will not emulate that misguided Pre-Raphaelite who sat down before a tree with intent to depict it leaf by leaf: for the seasons overtook him. We will further assume the foliage to be green, and the artist not to be colour-blind either congenitally or on a theory of his own. He squeezes out and mixes a pigment, green, on his palette, with some subsidiary pigments, by one or other to indicate the play of sunlight and shadow, and he sets to work, the result being the image of a tree. To be sure, the film producer may one day beat him by some coloured photograph of the tree springing from the soil, budding, expanding, harbouring birds' nests, shedding a series of annual leafage, growing to a monarch of the forest—all in twenty minutes. But let us, talking here to-day of 'imitation', imitate Isaak Walton's milkmaid, who

THE HANDICAP OF POETRY

cast away care and 'had not yet attained so much age and wisdom as to load her mind with any fears of many things that will never be', and particularly the fear that any mechanism can ever supersede in value man's individual brain and hand. There, if he paint, lies one advantage of his over the poet. He can, by pencil and colour, reproduce a vision which is almost immediately recognisable as a definite image; or, if more slowly, as a suggestive image: and he can do it *at one remove*.

IV

The poet works in words: and words—especially written words—are but hieroglyphics. If in verse, for instance, you or I wish to indicate that same green tree, we have to write down the word in a convention of alphabetical signs. How does the disposition of four letters G-R-E (doubled)-N resemble any visible colour preferable to any disposition of another four B-L-U-E? How by nature is T-R-E-E distinguished from B-U-S-H? Nay, to descend to our poor selves, how do we separate, save by symbols, our nightingales from our owls, our Ph.D.'s from our simple M.A.'s? We must colour them: we must fall back on the textile art: with its immediate vivid impression. All that Poetry, even, can present, must be presented by these words, symbols, tokens, hieroglyphics, and presented, as compared with painting, *at a second remove*—on the face of it, if I may invent the word, a most *dullifying* remove.

It would seem to follow, then, that in representing a scene, or in portraying a human being, poetry (and indeed all literature) is heavily handicapped by having to produce its effect through this *second remove*. Nor does its apparent disadvantage end here. A picture flashes itself upon the optic nerve, the one pinpoint of our nervous system which Nature exposes to the light: and the flash is carried straight to the brain. A poem, even when read or recited (as we may suppose Homer himself chanting it in a chief's hall or to a ring of the maids of Delos), made its way first through the tortuous passage of the ear to the brain (and you all know how much more slowly sound travels than light); had to be communicated from brain to the imaginative eye; and then travel back to the brain; before the hearer visualised the ships, the shore, the plain, the towers, old Chryses stalking along the edge of the surf, Achilles erect over the trench. Pass this delay of the ear and come to the words of Poetry, set down in writing or print. Consider the processes of reading, in their succession—the eye deciphering the hieroglyphics through training in an alphabet, translation dumbly to the ear, or to the brain; back to the eye which—more or less at the back of itself—has to translate the word into a new sort of vision and return it to the brain already surcharged as a clearing house with translating the language which the relentless bard continues to pour in upon it.

Add to this the difficult block of traffic at either end. The bard (unless he be gifted—as maidens in my part of the world are reputed to be—with the skill to pronounce 'scarlet geranium' as one syllable) has to filter out his words one by one, whether through the barrier of his

THE HANDICAP OF POETRY 109

teeth or in the single dribble of print: passing out his regiment of thought in single file, to be re-formed in our minds on the other side of the gateway.

Add yet another heavy weight to the handicap. The appeal of pictorial art is not only quick and direct, but universal. Any one of us can recognise even the scratchings of a prehistoric cave-man upon a bone as meant to represent something—an elk, let us say—that he was striving to represent. Very likely he would anticipate, under public criticism by his tribe, the answer given by Don Quixote's painter to those who interrupted his work with a demand to know what, precisely, he was depicting—'that, Señors, is as it may turn out'. He knew what he meant: and roughly, after these centuries and making allowance for his rudimentary implements and unpractised hand, *we* know what he meant. Nay, suppose this cave-man whisked forward on a magic carpet and set down before a Victorian canvas, say Frith's 'Paddington Station', cannot you see the adventurous fellow, while bewildered, yet enraptured, at once recognising the crowd on the platform as human beings of a far-dwelling tribe dressed up for some jamboree, jaunt, joy-ride, and wondering how many of his cattle (or wives) the priest would take in exchange for an excursion ticket? To speak more seriously—Almost any of us, two years ago, visiting the Persian Exhibition at Burlington House, could appreciate the beauty in design, colour, texture, of a Persian carpet. Many of us could instantly, without expert knowledge, take the impression of a Persian painting. How few of us have the *apparatus* to take in a dozen words of a Persian poem.

Here is the disability of varying language, commonly called the curse of Babel: and my friend (as I reminded you), the Professor of Poetry at Oxford, has said some very sensible things about this admitted nuisance.

V

I have indicated, then, three of Poetry's most obvious disabilities (there are others) as a rival of her sister, Painting. They are—to summarise—

(1) Her impression on the brain has to be slower and more intricate because it has to be conveyed by hieroglyphics, and interpreted at a remove which is, at least, secondary.

(2) It has to be conveyed in a thin succession of words, which must be accurately re-formed into their meaning by the hearer or reader.

(3) The regiments of words belong to so many nations, and are filed out through so many exits, that scarce one of us can deal with more than three or four.

VI

Let us now take these disabilities in reverse order.

To begin then with—(1) the old trouble about the Tower of Babel. Are the differences of speech among the tribes of men quite such a curse as we by habit assume them to be? A commercial traveller would at once answer 'yes', and with all his heart. To him in foreign trade some language like Esperanto would save much time and trouble, even as it would have saved an old grave Phoenician time and gesticulation when on the beach he undid his corded bales and

> Shy traffickers the dark Iberians came—

less shy when they read his goods priced in a universal alphabet. But I suggest, for your reflection, that the subtler thought of man in philosophy or, blent with emotion, in poetry, or in both aspiring to something *priceless*, cannot be standardised to a hard metal currency and made one medium of exchange.

I admit all the advantages that might accrue to us from a universal language, not only commercially—for I am not speaking to a commercial audience—but internationally, as helping us to that understanding of foreign minds which would seem invaluable in our present phase of history. I have a deep respect for all who would bring one nation closer to another by simplifying their speech.

But in the first place can it be done without imposition on liberty of thought while the thoughts of man, in his families, move on ways so subtly divergent, and he puts them into language the less translatable the more it is refined?

There lies the difficulty, with the endless temptation, for any of us who would translate, say an ode of Pindar or any ten lines of Virgil, into English. The more deeply one understands the original the more deeply he will despair of the result.

I suggest to you then that we do not too hastily echo the curse upon Babel, or pine or hope for Poetry written in some form of Esperanto. It is, if you remember, a part of Homer's testimonial to Odysseus that he had 'seen many cities of men and known their minds'—their several minds, mark you, subtly expressing themselves in the tongues they talked. As Don Quixote with his divine simplicity put it, arguing with the Man in Green—

> The great Homer wrote not in Latin because he was a Greek, and Virgil wrote not in Greek because he was a Latin. In brief, the poets of old wrote in the tongue they sucked in with their mothers' milk.

I suggest to you, Gentlemen (I say), in the first place, that these differences of language—man's divinest gift—may by their very diversity, more surely than by short cuts, lead to reconciliation in the end: that is, when we all agree to seek truth and if—as it may be—truth, like the Panther of Dante's quest, have its lair in no particular City though its scent be traceable in all. To a Frenchman, for example, the word *Patrie* carries with it a thrill which 'Our Country' does not quite convey to us. To an Englishman—far Colonist though he be—the word *Home* conveys a passion for which the Frenchman has not even a word in his dictionary, speak it nakedly as you will:

> Home, sweet home—
> *Douce Chez nous.*

It won't do. On no pair of scales will they balance.

But apart from this—(2) I ask you where would be all the accumulated treasures of human speech if Aeschylus, Virgil, Shakespeare had all used one common language reducible to some few hundreds of words? To take English alone—would you really rejoice in the

THE HANDICAP OF POETRY

scrapping of all that 'God's plenty' comprised in the New English Dictionary? A Society formed itself the other day to reduce our mother tongue to what it called 'Basic English'—that is, to provide (in the words of its own propaganda) a Universal Language whose vocabulary can be learnt in a few days. It started, very rightly, with an experiment—a translation of a German story into the sort of language it aimed at, and most cleverly (I admit) this was done. It prefaced the experiment with a list of these 'basic' words. Well, it is always an effort to tackle a list with any such claim. But it occurred to me, pondering it, to test it by nine simple words of Shakespeare, broken but most beautiful. You remember how, at the close of the famous soliloquy in the third act of *Hamlet*, Ophelia enters, a book of hours in her hand, and Hamlet greets her—

> Nymph, in thy Orisons
> Be all my sins remembered.

Now 'nymph' is a gracious word, calling up to the mind's eye the flash of many remembered visions from poetry, paintings, even surmises of our own past days. Browning, translating Euripides, preferred to write it 'numph' and possibly there are ladies who better correspond with that spelling. Anyhow I found neither 'nymph' nor 'numph' in the Basic Vocabulary. 'Orisons' I did not expect, nor was it there. 'Prayers', as an alternative? No! But I did look—in a Basic Vocabulary—to find 'sins'. No, not even sins.... 'What, no "sins"?' So he died, and she very imprudently married the Esperantist.

On this point lastly we must acknowledge that the Greeks, with all their wonderful discoveries in science and achievement in literature, had no language but their own. Yet, considering what the other nations have done since them, should we, as heirs of this expanded world, shrink from acknowledging that the very diversity of human thought, as expressed through various tongues, has added immeasurably to its total value?

VII

Now for the second handicap of Literature as against Painting. The speaker or writer must dribble out his words one by one, whereas the painter shows his canvas and we take in the picture in a moment.

Well, actually, we do not—quite: and the more we know about painting the less we do it. But, roughly, we may accept the distinction or series of distinctions which Lessing jotted down and left as preparatory notes for a second and third part of *Laocoon*, or maybe for a revision of Part I.

Painting makes use of figures and colours in *space*. Poetry of articulate sounds in *time*.

The signs of Painting are natural: those of Poetry are arbitrary—or, if you will, conventional hieroglyphics—G-R-E-E-N for instance the nearest it can get to representing that actual visible colour.

And (says he) 'the true end of any fine art can only be that which it is capable of arriving at without the help of another': and again 'I maintain that the true end of an art can only be that for which it is peculiarly and alone fit': and he quotes Plutarch as asking 'Who

THE HANDICAP OF POETRY

would split wood with a key, or open a door with an axe?'

Well, I shall try to show you, by-and-by, that Lessing's hardy pronouncement needs a good deal of qualification; is even an instance of galloping an aesthetic theory into the thickset of *what the poets wrote*. But (since we are practitioners in criticism) you may take it for a useful warning against poetry which aims at mere depiction, striving with words to embellish something stationary, vivid, demanding quick perception, better rendered by the brush; against the root-mistake of Darwin's *Botanic Garden*, for example: of painting the streaks of a tulip (as Johnson put it), of such lines as—

> There does the noble Gentian raise his head;
> Here creeps a lowly plant like some grey mist,
> Its leaves by nature shaped as cruciform....

Or, more philosophically,

> Here may the nice and curious eye explore
> How Nature's hand adorns the rushy moor:
> Here the rare moss in secret shade is found;
> Here the sweet myrtle of the shaking ground;[1]
> Beauties are these that from the view retire,
> But well repay th' attention they require.

We can all, at this time of day, detect the false bottom of that kind of poetry. But, since the purpose of these lectures is to drive at practice, and learn through concrete examples, let me instance for you the way in which a great (though loose) artist, Walter Scott, learned to improve on himself in the matter of *depicting* a young

[1] Bog-myrtle, that is.

woman, his heroine. *Waverley* was published in 1814, and in *Waverley*, to omit other roundabout talk of her, this is how Scott sets to work to present Rose Bradwardine. 'The Rose of Tully-Veolan'—

> She was indeed a very pretty girl of the Scotch type of beauty, that is, with a profusion of hair of pale gold, and a skin like the snow of her own mountains in whiteness. Yet she had not a pallid or pensive cast of countenance: her features, as well as her temper, had a lively expression; her complexion, though not florid, was so pure as to seem transparent, and the slightest emotion sent her whole blood at once to her face and neck. Her form, though under the common size, was remarkably elegant, and her motions light, easy and un-embarrassed. She came from another part of the garden to receive Captain Waverley, with a manner that hovered between bashfulness and courtesy.

But I suggest that with all this she was keeping Captain Waverley (as he might excusably have put it) the deuce of a time before allowing him to fall in love at first sight: and how on earth was he, happy fellow, to anticipate that the slightest emotion would send her whole blood at once into her face and neck? The passage in short is a mix-up of portrait and explanation: a hybrid attempt to combine two arts. It drags, and as a catch on the trigger, drags most fatally.

Pass four years in which Scott was learning the business which he might have learnt earlier from Fielding, and come to 1818, to *Rob Roy* and Diana Vernon. She flashes into the vision of a hunting-field—

> It was a young lady, the loveliness of whose very striking features was enhanced by the animation of the chase and the glow of the exercise, mounted on a beautiful horse, jet black,

THE HANDICAP OF POETRY

unless where he was flecked by spots of the snow-white foam which embossed his bridle. She wore, what was then something unusual, a coat, vest and hat, resembling those of a man....

You see the business proceeds, as in our experience, Gentlemen—or perhaps I should say in your experience—I hope it may proceed and develop. A vision of a beautiful girl on a horse—the man's eye, after a general impression, first on the horse, then on the daring unusual riding-habit, and then—and then the story goes off, as good stories should, at a gallop. And, as with portraiture, so with scenery. As a general rule in writing, to describe a scene at length and statically and then plant your moving actors against that background is a mistake, the better way is to introduce it through your actors' own eyes, as they see it: when, for example, your hero makes landfall of a strange coast you do not run ahead of him and paint the coast as a set-piece for his reception; since by so doing you would both check the movement and by anticipation spoil the wonder.

The way I recommend to you is as ancient as Homer, who (as Lessing observed) does not in the *Iliad* weary with any long description of the finished shield of Achilles but coaxes us up to the forge of Hephaestus, so that like the children at the open door of Longfellow's village smithy we see the work shaping under the workman's hammer, and—forgive the trite old verse—

> love to see the flaming forge
> And hear the bellows roar,
> And catch the burning sparks that fly
> Like chaff from a threshing-floor.

It is Homer's way in the *Odyssey*, too, where the Wanderers, *and we with them*, make landfall—

> on the foam
> Of perilous seas, in faery lands forlorn

and beach the black ship and disembark and wonder at cliff, glade and waterfall, we wondering (that is) through their eyes.

I assume you to be acquainted with that famous passage in *Lear* where Edgar leads Gloucester over the Kentish down and pretends to have brought him to the very edge of Dover cliff, from which the poor blind man would cast himself. The passage you perhaps have by heart. But anyway consider it.

A scene, fictitious, had to be described to a blind man—a scene of terrifying height, and so described that it communicates a terrific vision and sensible dizziness to the blind. How does Shakespeare make Edgar do it? Continuously: the height gradually indicated by depth.

At first the cliff-haunting birds, winging out far below in mid-air.

Then the eye is drawn back with a shudder to the sheer cliff, to the samphire-gatherer at his dreadful trade, he diminished to the size of his head, the fishermen on the beach beneath him to mice, the 'tall anchoring' bark off the beach to her cock boat, her cock boat again to a buoy 'almost too small for sight'. And then, sound travelling so much more slowly, last of all, even the surge

> The murmuring surge
> That on the unnumbered idle pebbles chafes
> Cannot be heard so high.

THE HANDICAP OF POETRY

So high anyhow that the recoil cannot wait for it.

> I'll look no more,
> Lest my brain turn, and the deficient sight
> Topple down headlong.

[Note by the way the subtle word 'deficient'—'deficient sight'—addressed to a blind man.] But mark generally how Edgar's vision is made to move, to diminish down, object by object, to scarcely a point, and scarcely a murmur of the surge rises so as to be audible.

VIII

This continuity of movement is the *first* redemption of literature from its handicap against painting. It has a competing vivacity of its own: it *goes* on: and merely by going on, it suggests life and challenges the *arrested moment* of any picture. Let the painter contrive that moment how he will—let him obey Lessing's advice and choose it to represent of an action neither the beginning nor the end but some midway point that throws the beholder's imagination at once backward, to reconstruct, and forward, to expect. Still the beholder does this with an effort: whereas without any realised effort our blood keeps pulsing on, carrying us through such time as is allotted us. While it keeps doing so we live: when it stops we die, and to this degree, no matter how vividly it seek to portray life, or how suggestively—be it a battle-scene, or the embrace of lovers, or the stir of leaves lifted by a passing wind—every painting must portray life *sub specie mortis*.

But literature enjoys another and far more considerable advantage over its sister art. I may indicate it by a sentence from a famous page of Landor's, though Landor is not speaking of literature or of poetry, but of the passage of human life. 'The present, like a note in music, is nothing but as it appertains to what is past and what is to come.' So it is with the hieroglyphics we call words. Nothing in themselves, they take an infinite flexibility of meaning from an infinite possible variety of settings; and not only that, but—since no two minds are alike—by Association of Ideas they command an infinite multiplicity of appeal.

FIRST AID IN CRITICISING. IV

WORDS AND NATURE

I

WE left off, Gentlemen, upon a sentence of Landor's—'The present, like a note in music, is nothing but as it appertains to what is past and what is to come'. I tore that sentence roughly—as we expositors do—out of his lovely dialogue between the slave Aesop and the slave-girl Rhodope: to which I hope you will resort and, resorting, let its cadences fall on your ears and dwell. If so dwelling, they pull you quite away from this room and the lecturer's voice, to forget it in a sudden awed surmise of what literature can do, why then the happier my chance: for you will be *feeling* the power of fine literature in communion with the thing itself. Believe me, I value these talks as nothing, but in so far as they help you towards clarifying that vision, so that by a little you train yourselves to discern and enjoy rightly. For all good literature (I think—for Poetry, I am certain) the first great step is to feel it, to respond to it, though for the moment you may not quite know how, or exactly why. 'It is a test', says Mr T. S. Eliot in his essay on Dante, '...that genuine poetry can communicate before it is understood'. Take *The Tempest*, for example, as it appeals to a boy—as I remember first reading it as a boy at the age of eight in a ditch into which I had been tumbled with a young sister and the first volume of Knight's *Shakespeare*, by a broken carriage-axle—the book a sudden wonder and a wild desire, continuing when the wheelwright arrived and my sister (adoring blacksmiths as all good children should) preferred his mechanics to Prospero's. A childish, ignorant enchantment, that of the boy; yet somehow, and just so, an initiation into a cult. To help that surmise to a wider understanding, without dulling the first ardour, or thumbing off its bloom—that is the almost impossible task laid upon teachers and professors. Will you bear this in mind and not resent it if our approach now and then seem too elementary?

II

To take up the parable, then—

A word in a sentence is not *quite* so insignificant taken by itself as a note of music taken by itself. A single quaver in the clef of G does not (I think) convey quite so much as the single hieroglyphic 'green' which at least calls up in the mind's eye a preparative impression though spoken or written alone. There are, to be sure, notes which struck separately and repeatedly on a single bell should, by Association of Ideas, remind many that the hour is near for going to Church. But that call is a repetition by convention, has nothing to do with the meaning of Music, and I suggest that we can for the moment disregard it as outside our argument.

Let us take the word G-R-E-E-N, 'green', and consider a few of the many meanings and shades of meaning it can take in collocation with other words that go before and after. Let us start with it in a broad, simple meaning—

> Robin is in the green wood gone...

—or, if you will, more particularly—

> In somer when the shawes be sheyne
> And leves be large and long,
> Hit is full merry in feyre forrest
> To here the foulys song.
>
> To se the dere draw to the dale
> And leve the hilles hie,
> And shadow hem in the leves grene
> Under the green-wode tree....
>
> Pluck up the herte, my dere mayster,
> Litulle Johne can say,
> And think hit is a full fayre tyme
> In a morning of May.

All quite simple as yet—'Under the Greenwood Tree, Who loves to lie with me, and turn his merry note unto the sweet bird's throat', as Amiens artificially sings it later: and yet charged with any number of historical meanings and undertones, if you consider what a winter meant in England in those days, especially to the poor: the stint of food and fodder: the windows unglazed therefore shuttered against the weather; hall and kitchen therefore dark day-long for months or lit only as Tom bore logs into the hall or a niggardly faggot stolen from the woods fed the labouring man's fire. No reading, no evening newspaper there: or, if you prefer it, suppose this lecture room full of icy draughts, wherein your feet kept shuffling in the straw, and coughing drowned the lecturer's saw, and Marion's nose—but no! Marion's nose had not intruded that much, as yet, into Cambridge, to compensate. So we will take up this word 'green' in collocation with 'a morning of May'—'May Morning'—the traditional anniversary fixed in the medieval mind, anticipating, may be prompting a little, God's goodness to release men from this many months' misery —as hope had fixed St Valentine's Day for the registry office of the birds to open. Let Dekker conclude on this simple note

> O, the month of May, the merry month of May,
>   So frolic, so gay and so green, so green, so green!
> O, and then did I unto my true love say,
>   Sweet Peg, thou shalt be my Summer's Queen.

—or, if you prefer to conclude on the note of '*Nous n'irons plus aux bois*'—

> You and I and Amyas,
> Amyas and you and I,
> To the greenwood must we go, alas!
> You and I, my lyf, and Amyas.

Now let us take the word and consider it as a note in some contexts of subtler significance. We are still in mere greenery with Marvell's——

> Annihilating all that's made
> To a green thought in a green shade:

but even here we are introducing thought as a shade of the colour—which we have not done as yet. Now see the word in Macbeth—

> No, this my hand will rather
> The multitudinous seas incarnadine,
> Making the green one red.

[Have you ever noted, by the way, how often—almost persistently—Shakespeare visualises the sea as *green*?

      'Twixt the green sea and the azured vault.
                                  [*The Tempest*]
          Of the sea-water green, Sir.
                              [*Love's Labour's Lost*]
and Antony's—   I, that with my sword
    Quarter'd the world, and o'er green Neptune's back
    With ships made cities.

The curve of a breaking wave, the translucent hollow under the crest of its foam being almost invariably green.]

Pass on to derivatives in meaning—'green youth' for young sprouting forwardness, 'green-eyed jealousy', etc., then back, if you will, to Shelley's

      Many a green isle needs must be
      In the deep wide sea of Misery

or back to 'green' as a word of locality, the 'wanton green' of fairyland, the village green with its cricketers, Blake's *Echoing Green* and so on.

III

Alongside with 'green' I instanced the word 'home'. The French have it not; nor the Italians (unless you count *dimora* which can miss our word in many shades of meaning): and this is strange in these Latin races, because the Latins themselves had something near to it in *domus*—as Wykehamists feel, all the world over, when they arise and sing their regimental '*Domum*'. A legend, you know (and it has significance), traces the authorship of that song to a poor boy marooned at Winchester while his school-fellows had flown off to their holidays—sometimes with the addition that he was chained to a tree! Well the *intelligentsia* Press is making great play, just now, with what it calls 'the Public School System', and quite a few little birds-errant are returning from the strawberries to defile their own several nests: but the system must have improved between then and now, when ninety-nine of every hundred past members of an ancient school will (as a historian has noted) convert into a Hymn of Devotion to *Alma Mater* a song composed to celebrate the delights of getting away from her.

But let that be. It must be obvious (I think) that this word 'home' contains, according as it is set with other words or suggests divers thoughts and emotions, a store of iridescence; a capacity to catch, reflect, animate more sudden, or awake deeper, meanings than lie within the range of so plain and obvious a word as 'green'. We may compare their difference in this respect, perhaps, with the difference between an emerald and a diamond. The one, by itself, is pure 'green', to be illuminated in ring or necklace by neighbour gems, or have its depth pierced by various lights: while the diamond catches and sheds light from its every facet, spends itself in distributing beauty, here, there and everywhere different —the *Sirius* of the gems.

So the word 'home', according as the poet sets it, may (if he be a bad poet) convey no more than does 'A Home from Home' on the advertisement of a 'Temperance Hotel'—that accurate translation but insanitary perversion of the noble toast οἴκοθεν οἴκαδε with which in Hellas a host would welcome a stranger, lifting the wine-cup. If the poet be a better one, he will make it reach far above that, very far above 'Mrs So-and-So, At Home, Fridays 4 to 6'—to express anything from infinite regret, or infinite rest, or infinite yearning: from simple nostalgia in the traveller to a mystic's ecstasy. For a sample or two—

> Home, dearie, home. O it's home I want to be!

> Here to thy bosom, and my home—

> I ken my home, and it affords some ease
> To see afar the smoking cottages—

> And as a hare, whom hounds and horns pursue
> Pants to the place from whence at first she flew,
> I still had hopes, my long vexations pass'd,
> Here to return, and die at home at last—

that by an Irishman. For a Scot, take Stevenson's poignant *Christmas at Sea*—the supposed speaker being a wastrel sailorman, almost wrecked in sight of the lit windows of the home from which he had run away to sea, but now clawing off the lee-shore against the gale:

O well I saw the pleasant room, the pleasant faces there,
My mother's silver spectacles, my father's silver hair....
But all that I could think of, in the darkness and the cold,
Was just that I was leaving home and my folks were growing old.

Pass that sentiment, or sentimentality of regret, and come to Waller—

> The soul's dark cottage, batter'd and decay'd,
> Lets in new light through chinks that Time hath made:
> Stronger by weakness, wiser men become
> As they draw near to their eternal home.

So much for resignation, hope. Now for one single instance of the word passed up from affection, sentiment, hope, to exaltation—

> Hierusalem, my happy *home*,
>   When shall I come to thee?
> When shall my sorrow have an end,
>   Thy joys when shall I see?...
>
> Thy gardens and thy gallant walks
>   Continually are *green*;
> There grow such sweet and pleasant flowers
>   As nowhere else are seen.
>
> Quite through thy streets, with silver sound
>   The flood of Life doth flow:
> Upon whose banks on every side
>   The wood of Life doth grow....
>
> Our Lady sings *Magnificat*
>   With tones surpassing sweet;
> And all the Virgins bear their part,
>   Sitting about her feet....
>
> Hierusalem, my happy *home*,
>   Would God I were in thee!
> Would God my woes were at an end,
>   Thy joys that I might see!

'Jerusalem', 'Sion', 'Home'—'If I forget thee, O Jerusalem', 'When we remembered thee, O Sion'.

> Nor shall my sword sleep in my hand
> Till we have built Jerusalem
> In England's green and pleasant land.

All the Women's Institutes singing together! At once the dear city and landscape of our nursery window and the Celestial City whose walls 'conjubilant in song... with carbuncles do shine'!

IV

I said 'nursery' windows. I should have said 'nurseries' and 'windows'. For that is the next point in my argument. The word 'home', which I have chosen as it chanced, not only takes and refracts a different tint of meaning as the poet sets it, but even, as so set, conveys by Association of Ideas a different meaning—different if slight—to every one of us in the degrees that our sense of Home has been deep or slight, happy or unhappy. As no two persons alive have precisely the same thumb-marks; as no two of our species carry under their hats precisely the same convolutions in the brain; so the word 'home' will carry some difference of meaning to each one of us, no matter how anxiously mothered, or on what landscape his nursery window opened—on what green fields with slow cattle, on what 'Satanic mills', on what visions of what fair land beyond—what inviting seas, what office-desks. No two men, probably, carry home the same impression from a spectacle—a Lord Mayor's Show or a Village Fair. You have, in dealing with any word in any setting, to take account of this immense power of literature, with its immense danger—that it affects every single reader, every single hearer, differently though it enlist—though it command —a multitude.

Further, you have to take into account that it not only commands each individual separately, but commands him differently at various stages of his growth. I began (and I hope not impertinently) by recalling the first spell of Shakespeare on a callow child. Well, one hopes to have acquired a deeper understanding of *The Tempest* since then. If that first feeble surmise has developed with these years, and its measure grown without diminishing the joy, surely a man may claim that *The Tempest* has followed him as a blessing through life. And here again Shakespeare shall serve me to put before you yet another virtuous and preservative herb in Literature. It not only adapts itself flexibly to millions of us in import, as we individually grow; it adapts itself to successive generations of men and is, to them in turn, prophetically if variously valuable.

Johnson, in the famous preface to his edition of Shakespeare, asserts of him in his solid way, that 'What mankind have long possessed they have often examined and compared; and if they persist to value the possession, it is because frequent comparisons have confirmed opinion in its favour....'. 'These plays (says he) have passed through variations of taste and changes of manners, and, as they devolved from one generation to another, have received new honours at every transmission.... The sand heaped by one flood is scattered by another, but the rock always continues in place. The stream of Time, which is continually washing the dissoluble fabricks of other poets, passes without injury by the adamant of Shakespeare.'

—Which is true enough, until we allow ourselves to be misled by the simile. Or, anyhow, let Shakespeare be the rock and we the adaptable generations carried past it. The point is that, accepting Shakespeare for supreme, succeeding generations have worshipped him for supremacies amazingly diverse—one for his easy spontaneous grace and 'native wood notes wild', another for his noble delineation of character, another for his moral edification, yet another for his 'acting quality' and to-day (I suppose) yet another again for his incomparable way of saying things—so getting back through men who—albeit worshippers—could hardly read his Sonnets if they were paid for it, to the very musical excellence of poetry he was attempting, feeling after, in *Venus and Adonis*.

V

And so, Gentlemen, with Shakespeare as my last instance, I come to this—the *vivacity* of Literature as an Art, and its vitality, which goes deeper and of which vivacity is the expression, may be traced to their source in that lively *continuous* jet of the blood for which, though other animals share it, man alone has been granted the divine gift of translating its joys and sorrows into articulate speech, and by articulate speech regimenting his brain to thought, and, by setting down his thoughts in writing not only memorising them for himself as pointers to further expanding thoughts, but, if they be memorable, transmitting them to others in the service of thoughts still breeding and multiplying. There has been wastage, lamentable wastage, from the beginning—through impercipience, or neglect—

> There may be cities that refuse
> To their own child the honours due,
> And look ungently on the Muse;
> But ever shall those cities rue

> The dry, unyielding niggard breast,
>   Offering no nourishment, no rest,
> To that young head which soon shall rise
>   Disdainfully, in might and glory, to the skies.

There has been wastage, through the sack of cities, loot or burning of libraries (from Alexandria to Louvain). Where are now the lost books of Livy? Where the comedies of those who, by Athenian vote, many times beat Aristophanes at his own game? Where are those easy, ill-written hundreds of pages which Shakespeare (to Jonson's annoyance) declined to blot, and passed on to be sliced up into actor's parts or to be spidered-over as prompt copies, to be rescued at any haphazard by Heminge and Condell and heaped for the labour of ages 'on pilèd stones'.—Well, with the help of photography we are insuring the perpetuity of the word in old manuscripts, as with cheap reproduction in print we are coping with the natural desiccation of wood-pulp, and renewing the material life of to-day's 'best sellers'.

VI

But—to recall ourselves to the philosophy of it—if our literature at all (as I have tried to argue) correspond to our life, which again answers the beat of our blood, we can move on another step and say that *rhythm* must be natural to it. For the moment let me say only that, if our blood starts beating irregularly, if our arteries refuse to function normally, the wise will call in a physician; and so I hold (merely warning you ahead of a later argument, that genius is not a burst of eccentricity, or the 'original'

WORDS AND NATURE

to be confused with the abnormal, but, rather, that genius lies in developing the normal, that which is healthy in us to its *n*th power)—that our human aspirations in Poetry, however elevated, will only be valuable as they can be called back to the well-spring of our blood within us. As Meredith says (and I think wisely) even of Prayer—

And let the prayer be as a fountain. Rising on a spout, from dread of the hollow below, the prayer may be prolonged in words begetting words, and have a pulse of fervour: the spirit of it has fallen after the first jet. That is the delirious energy of our craving, which has no life in our souls. We do not get to Heaven by renouncing the Mother we spring from: and when there is an eternal secret for us, it is best to believe that Earth knows it, to keep near her, even in our utmost aspirations.

Now on this question of *rhythm*, as a natural instinct in the poet as answering, little or more as he be aware of it, to the rhythmical pulse of the blood within his own body, little or more as he surmise that responsive, unheard, beat in each single one of his audience, let me say a word or two. In the *Poetics* Aristotle lets fall a seemingly casual sentence which the commentators have usually passed over as negligible. 'Imitation', he says, 'being natural to us—as also the sense of harmony and rhythm, *the metres being obviously species of rhythms* —it was through their original aptitude, and by a series of improvements for the most part gradual at first, that men created poetry out of their improvisations.' In the *Rhetoric* he qualifies this with a warning almost equally worth your attention, especially when you come to deal with prose. 'Prose Composition', he says in effect, 'should be neither metrical nor altogether devoid of measure or rhythm. When applied to the affairs of common life, an accomplished metrical structure makes a composition unnatural.' (Let us, for instance, consider Pope's *Essay on Man* as a touchstone for that remark.) Aristotle goes on—'The manifest artificiality totally deprives it of all truth and reality, of all power to move the feelings and induce conviction. Concurrently it diverts the attention of the hearers, who, instead of holding their minds on the business, are waiting for the recurrence of your rhythm: just as children in the market-place anticipate the recurrent cry of'—well for Aristotle's instance let us substitute "All the Winners!"

VII

Pupils and readers of mine must be well aware—perhaps are well weary—of my old insistence that in some interpretation of Platonic harmony must lie the secret of the Universe and of life itself; and, if of life on this planet, then of poetry, taking it with the ultra-Newtonian law that spirit attracts spirit as surely as matter attracts matter. I insist on it because I believe in it, because it compels and conquers me by its noble simplicity: and, believing, I must use the modicum of wit and the platform granted me to proclaim it—here and now—as the principle of Poetry, because ultimately the principle of religion and of love.

We have seen in our day many marvels that 'Applied Science' has commanded and brought to our doors, and I doubt not that in time it will harness the tides of Ocean to serve us. But the science of which I speak is a *Scientia scientiarum*. It transcends utility. Yet maybe man will find its use—in teaching him to know himself and his place, abating his self-conceit.

VIII

A sensible man does not aspire to bind the sweet influences of Pleiades: or loosen the bands of Orion: but he may, and does, aspire to understand something of the universal harmony in which he and they bear a part, if only that he may render it a more perfect obedience. 'Let me know', he craves, 'that I may accept my fate intelligently, even though it prove that under the iron rule of Necessity I have no more freedom of will than the dead,

> Roll'd round in earth's diurnal course
> With rocks, and stones, and trees.

The claim (as Man must think) is a just one—for why was he given intelligence if not to use it? And even though disallowed as presumptuous, it is an instinctive one. Man *is*, after all, a part of the Universe, and just as surely as the Pleiades or Arcturus: and moreover he *feels* in himself a harmony correspondent with the greater harmony of his quest. His heart beats to a rhythm: his blood pulses through steady circuits; like the plants by which he is fed, he comes to birth, grows, begets his kind, dies, and returns to earth; like the tides, his days of gestation obey the moon and can be reckoned by her; in the sweat of his body he tills the ground, and by the seasons, summer and winter, seed and harvest, his life while it lasts is regulated. But above all he is the microcosm, the tiny percipient centre upon which the immense cosmic circle focusses itself as the sun upon a burning-glass—and he is not shrivelled up by the miracle! Other creatures (he notes) share his sensations; but, so far as he can discover, not his intelligence—or, if at all, in no degree worth measuring. So far as he can detect, he is not only an actor in the grand pageant, but the sole intelligent spectator.

Also in his daily life Man is for ever seeking after harmony in avoidance of chaos, cultivating personal habits after the clock; in his civic life forming governments, attempting hierarchies, laws, constitutions, by which (as he hopes) a system of society will sometime work in tune. When he fights he has learnt that his fighting men shall march in rhythm and deploy rhythmically. If he haul rope or weigh anchor, setting out to sea, or haul up his ship on a beach, he has proved by experiment that these operations are performed more than twice as easily when done to a tune. But these are dull, less than half-conscious, imitations of the great harmony for which, when he starts out to understand and interpret it consciously, he must use the most godlike of all his gifts. Now the most godlike of all human gifts—the singular gift separating Man from the brutes—is speech. If he can harmonise speech he has taught his first and peculiar faculty to obey the great rhythm: 'I will sing and give praise', says the Psalmist, 'with the best member that I have'. Thus by harmonising speech he arrives at *Poetry*, and so a step nearer to the meaning of Nature.

PATERNITY IN SHAKESPEARE

I

FIFTY YEARS and more have gone by since the first appearance in print of Maine's *Ancient Law*, now an accepted classic. It arrived in 1861, cleaving the fog (so to speak) like Athene's galley: and although in the later years of Victoria's reign some mist of doubt followed and overtook the gallant vessel in port and, in the words of Sir Frederick Pollock, his later and learned editor, clever young men went about saying that by McLennan or Morgan, one or other, Maine had been exploded—well, all classics invite that fate, as to survive the test approves them classical.

As a layman in the law then, and for his purpose this afternoon, your lecturer may be allowed to assume that Maine's famous Fifth Chapter on the growth of Social Law out of Patriarchal Custom, the legal affirmation of this in the *Patria Potestas*, with later modifications, lawyers' fictions and inventions to make the system elastic as families dwindled while the nation expanded, holds its authority.

So, to start my argument by telling you what you know already—even as Orlando starts the argument of *As You Like It* by confiding, 'As I remember, Adam, it was upon this fashion—bequeathed me by will but poor a thousand crowns', etc.—let me try to condense Maine's thesis into a sentence or two. Whatever may have happened among other races, among those we separate and classify under the term 'Indo-European' social order derives, so far back as can be traced, from the Family, with its Father as head, lawgiver, justiciar, administrator of its possessions. In ancient policy this is not yet law as we understand it, being older than any writing and therefore older than any code. But it is Custom, the rule of the Patriarch, filially binding. The Mother, if imported from another tribe, is but an adjunct; if of the same tribe, yet but a servant over lesser servants as proud mother of the legitimate children, of whom the eldest male even remains a servant while his father lives and for misconduct can be sold into slavery by an incensed father's will. At this point the question of marriage, whether by barter or capture, simply does not come in. If I quote Professor Malinowski's concluding sentence on *Marriage* in the fourteenth edition of the *Encyclopaedia Britannica*—

Marriage, like most problems of anthropology, is ceasing to be a subject of speculation and becoming one of empirical research

—it is simply to support that general truth from personal observation.

II

But I am concerned here to note, for the moment only and for my purpose, how the emotion of ancient poetry supports Maine. The father yearns over the son, his first-born, his successor: the son would save his father above all possessions. Priam goes by night through enemy lines to plead for Hector's body. Aeneas is 'pious' persistently for having borne Anchises out on

PATERNITY IN SHAKESPEARE 139

his back through the flames of Troy. Orestes has to slay his mother for having murdered his father, and on legal grounds is acquitted for it by the Areopagus. Oedipus suffers the worst for having, without his knowing, slain an unfatherly father in a roadside scuffle—the sort of homicide in which nowadays Oedipus would probably be the victim and Laius in his car covered by third-party risks. (And Oedipus did it in the very act of avoiding that prophecy of parricide with which the Oracle was haunting him.) Turn to the Hebrews and their Scriptures—through Genesis and its patriarchal system, right up and through Mosaic Law, in legend, history, song, this writ of the father runs, with the concurrent testimony and support of paternal or filial affection. What passage in the Old Testament so moving as that of David seated between the gates, watching the road, turning the messengers of victory aside for news of Absalom, guilty of all unfilial crimes? Or in the Gospel what parable of Jesus so poignant as that of the Prodigal Son? And how does Saint Paul (himself a lawyer) sum up this fatherly, this answering filial στοργή but thus?—that the spirit of the creature yearneth after the spirit of the Creator:

> The Spirit itself beareth witness with our spirit that we are the children of God:
> And if children, then heirs....
> For we have received the spirit of adoption, whereby we cry 'Abba, Father'.

Throwing still farther back and east to Persia, we find this same parental στοργή or 'yearning of the bowels' in the tragedy of Sohrab and Rustum. But I must hurry on; for there is still a traject to be crossed between all this and Shakespeare.

III

I must hasten past the entrance, paying out my all-too-few coins. To pass to Rome, then, we know the peculiarly horrible death of the man convicted of parricide. Later, when Christianity conquered, in its historical way, by absorbing, digesting, adapting to its spiritual purpose this, that and the other of the cults, laws, observances it superseded, it would seem to have assumed this terrible sanctity of Fatherhood into the Hebraic conception of God, the unknown invisible Father. This conception of Him, whether as omnipotent or even as all-merciful (since nothing, even though it be a chance of mercy, terrifies man like the unknown), while it ennobled God, increased man's awe. It is therefore significant that through the darkest of what we conveniently call the Dark Ages, while the Christian faith was penetrating through tribes of men whose pagan inherited impulse was to materialise every spiritual concept and personify every notion of a deity, no artist dared to depict God the Father. He might be represented as an Eye with the word 'Jehovah', or a script 'I Am', penetrating clouds in a shaft of light; or later, on such a ray, a bird descending as the LOGOS to the Virgin's ear—interpenetration of the soul through celestial speech.

IV

The easing of this awful veneration of the invisible Father seems to have come about through the rise of what we now call 'Mariolatry'. Just how the worship of the Virgin sprang up, grew, dominated, I am not learned enough to tell. Possibly it started with the Gnostics and their theory of a female *Sophia* as a feminine emanation of the deity, helped perhaps by the Church's need of providing an ideal of chastity for women, to balance its ideal of monkish abstinence, saintly mortifications of the flesh, for men. Gnosticism, anyhow, was not so much a Christian heresy as the challenge of another cult—if one may use the single term 'cult' of a thing so varying with its various professors, that almost one may describe it as a Neo-Platonic pawnshop crowded with pagan deposits, old vestments, 'articles of bigotry and virtue'. Indeed, its stock seems to have changed hands so often that one can hardly call it a 'cult', still less a 'sect'; as Dean Inge puts it, 'Gnosticism is the name, not of a sect, but of a tendency'. It was a large and many-sided movement, which was continually changing; and the Church, always more tender towards alien inventions—always, so to speak, more easy-going with its imports than with its exports—admitted this doctrine to improve on it, and in time to lift and build it in as the head of a corner, facing Christ.

But here let me quote a passage you will rightly listen to with more respect than to any words of mine. It is Lecky who speaks:

The world is governed by its ideals, and seldom or never has there been one which has exercised a more profound and, on the whole, a more salutary influence than the medieval conception of the Virgin. For the first time woman was elevated to her rightful position, and the sanctity of weakness was recognised, as well as the sanctity of sorrow. No longer the slave or toy of man, no longer associated only with ideas of degradation and sensuality, woman rose, in the person of the Virgin Mother, into a new sphere, and became the object of a reverential homage of which antiquity had had no conception. Love was idealised. The moral charm and beauty of female excellence were fully felt. A new type of character was called into being: a new kind of admiration was fostered. Into a harsh and ignorant and benighted age this ideal type infused a conception of gentleness and of purity unknown to the proudest civilisations of the past. In the pages of living tenderness which many a monkish writer has left in honour of his celestial patron, in the millions who, in many lands and in many ages, have sought with no barren desire to mould their characters into her image, in those holy maidens who, for the love of Mary, have separated themselves from all the glories and pleasures of the world, to seek in fastings and vigils and humble charity to render themselves worthy of her benediction, in the new sense of honour, in the chivalrous respect, in the softening of manners, in the refinement of tastes displayed in all the walks of society: in these and in many other ways we detect its influence. All that was best in Europe clustered around it, and it is the origin of many of the purest elements of our civilisation.

So far Lecky: and we may memorise the gist of it, if we will, in six lines of Mary Coleridge:

> Blue is Our Lady's colour,
> White is Our Lord's.
> To-morrow I will wear a knot
> Of blue and white cords,
> That you may see it, where I ride
> Among the flashing swords.

'But', Lecky adds, 'the price, and perhaps the necessary price, of this was the exaltation of the Virgin as an omnipresent deity of infinite power as well as of infinite condescension': and (if I may take up the familiar tale to condense it into a few words necessary to the argument) this ideal of Divine Motherhood, with its offspring in chivalry, provoked revolt by excess, and gathered a variety of enemies with a fine confusion of attack to match the fertility of its devotees' invention. The earnest Reformer or Protestant, bent on direct access to God the Father, searching his Bible for it doggedly, himself dogged by suspicion of Rome and Rome's intermediary glosses, found no warrant that Mary was actually God's Bride and authoritative 'Queen of Heaven'; while, looking on the world about him, he saw idolatry in the images of her and a pullulating host of minor Saints with their miracle-working relics and the trade in them. The scholars of the Revival of Learning easily detected that much of this idolatry was but old polytheism revived. Take the famous passage from Erasmus' story of the Shipwreck, of the sailors calling on the Virgin and the Saints and promising candles. 'But what has Our Lady to do with this affair?'—'Well, you see', comes the answer; 'of old, Venus looked after mariners because she was believed to be born of the sea; and since she has gone out of the business, the Virgin Mother was put in place of her who was a mother though not a Virgin.' The thrust, so delicate, is deadly—deep as a well if not so wide as a church door—and it serves, drawing after it the blood that marks the place for Luther's hatchet. After this Don Quixote, with his Dulcinea del Toboso, becomes only a question of time.

Meanwhile, be it noted, in the Law—to which all questions of inheritance must appeal—and in the accepted practice of the Courts, the old Roman tradition of *Patria Potestas* remains paramount. Through the sire the blood derives its title, its name: and in the often-quoted words of Chief-Justice Crewe:

> I suppose there is no man that hath any apprehension of gentry or nobleness but his affection stands to the continuance of a noble name and house, and would take hold of a twig or twine-thread to uphold it.

On top of all this, of course, and on the heels of the New Learning, comes in the Italianate cult of *virtù*; of the unbridled male, let loose to exploit his will and self to the *n*th term; in learning or lust, in experiment, exploration, discovery on sea and land, piracy, political intrigue with dagger at the hip and poison in the closet, bargains with Satan and death defied in the high Roman manner (as interpreted by Seneca)—yet Death dissected with a peculiar fascination for detail and its naked horrors—all a most fruitful field for loud rhetoric and dramatic passion: since, as pointed out by Aristotle (whose *Poetics*, lately exhumed, had rapidly become a text-book), Drama exhibits persons 'doing things': and men in that age were 'doing things' with a vengeance.

V

Doubtless it would have astonished the several members of the mixed English crew whose ghosts we have been summoning if anyone had informed them that they were all pulling away from Mariolatry in the same boat. Certainly they bear little resemblance to Andrew Marvell's crew, communally singing by the remote Bermudas

> in an English boat
> A holy and a cheerful note;
> And all the way to guide their chime
> With falling oars they kept the time.

The sturdy Protestant would little guess that an Italianate Englishman, 'a devil incarnate', was backing his stroke; or the lawyer at No. 6, who kept his eyes in the boat, that the fellow behind him was a play-actor whose thwart by rights should be the stocks; or that an alchemist was somewhere up in the bows. And the steerswoman was a Virgin Queen and Defender of the Faith whom somehow, though she might accept any amount of pastoral eulogy, it was extremely hard to mistake for the *Rosa sine Spina*, that other Virgin. Still, and anyhow, the woman knew how to steer—to handle the tiller-lines around bends and through currents, and —what is more—to command her crew to 'sit' the Royal Barge from Windsor down; with liberty, after she had alighted at Westminster, to disembark, still lower down, at Traitor's Gate. Especially hard would it be for the Puritan to recognise the help of the playwright, whom he actively detested and denounced. But the playwright is (or in those days I should say *was*) no propagandist. He reflects the spirit of his age alike because he shares it and because his audience demands it. I dare say that amid the vast literature piled upon and around Shakespeare there may exist some monumental work treating this idea of paternity; from the personification of God the Father in *Everyman*, and the fatherly vengeance of *The Spanish Tragedy*, down through Shakespeare and the whole line of his successors. If such a treatise exist, forgive in what follows the freshness of unaided surmises operating upon ignorance.

VI

Anyhow, I am committed to talk of Shakespeare, and of his treatment of Paternity.

To begin with the Comedies, and with the heroines: their wonderful and constantly fresh adornment. Have you realised that *scarcely a one of them has a mother*; or if she have, has no mother that counts? Search the *dramatis personae*. Julia and Silvia have no mothers. The Princess and her ladies in *Love's Labour's Lost* have no mothers. Hermia and Helena in *A Midsummer Night's Dream* have no mothers. Sweet Anne Page has a mother, to be sure, but one who would marry her to an old man she detests, while her father insists upon a man she despises; and it is the lover of her choice who spirits her away from between them:

> 'Which means she to deceive, father or mother?'
> 'Both, my good host, to go along with me....'

Hero and Beatrice have no mothers: a star danced and Beatrice was born. Rosalind and Celia have no mothers. Portia has no mother. Isabella of course has no mother. Katharina and Bianca in *The Shrew* have no mothers, Helena in *All's Well* has no mother, Viola has no mother. Perdita grows up without a mother;

PATERNITY IN SHAKESPEARE

and so Marina; and so again Miranda, who, forced to search back memory to a dim time when she was three years old, can only answer:

>'Tis far off;
>And rather like a dream than an assurance
>That my remembrance warrants. Had I not
>Four or five women once that tended me?

In sum all these maidens, so variously charming, have not a mother among them, to give counsel. Husband-high, they will win husbands in their own way, being wooed or wooing.

In the Historical Plays, of course, Shakespeare's invention is constrained by his material; history having to record what eminent men actually did or suffered. We may suppose that in the history of England from John to Henry VIII he *might* have found women to voice the maternal στοργή otherwise than do the Lady Constance, cursing, and the three mothers (one his own) who successively pour curses on Richard the Third. Somehow he did not.

We turn to the Tragedies. As a specimen of motherhood (you will agree) Queen Tamora in *Titus Andronicus* is not to be commended. The mother in *Cymbeline* is a stepmother and behaves 'as such' and more so. Lady Capulet is of no help at all to her daughter. The only women in *Timon* are two strumpets. And what is the real meaning in *Troilus* of—'Think! we had mothers!'? There is no mother in *Julius Caesar*; but there is mention of one—from whom Cassius got his bad temper— or so he avers. Cressida has no mother. Desdemona has no mother. Ophelia has no mother, poor soul, and,

148 PATERNITY IN SHAKESPEARE

for lack of one to confess to and be advised, is pestered with sententious talk, by a prig of a brother and a fool of a father. Cordelia has no mother. (But of *Hamlet* and *Lear* I shall speak by and by.) Lady Macbeth has been a mother, and how does she recall it in the leap of her ambition?—

> I have given suck, and know
> How tender 'tis to love the babe that milks me:
> I would, while it was smiling in my face,
> Have plucked my nipple from his boneless gums
> And dash'd the brains out, had I sworn as you
> Have done to this.

—after which it seems something of an anticlimax to observe that Cleopatra has no mother, though it may amuse us to imagine one, and speculate on what would have happened to her had she interfered in the drama.

Against all this will anyone weigh Volumnia pleading as a Roman mother for Rome and in her pride of him persuading Coriolanus to his death? No, that may be history, and true: yet, to my mind, is more Roman than motherly. Or shall we count for much those two pretty, pathetic nursery scenes, in which Hermione and Lady Macduff are prattled to by their pretty sons? They go but a little way, I fear, towards filling that absence of motherhood in the Plays which I, for one, feel as a sensible void, and passing strange.

VII

But now let us turn to the fathers in these plays and consider them for a few minutes.

I shall not stress the disproportionate amount of

PATERNITY IN SHAKESPEARE

room they occupy in the playbills; though that is significant, as I hope the earlier part of my argument has shown. The preponderance of males is not Shakespearian at all: it cannot even be pressed as specially significant in any European drama of that age (though it might be amusing to count the number of male characters in the corpus of that Drama, divide it by the number of women, and reflect on the quotient); the inequality being as old as Drama itself, and naturally in all ages which agree that the province of man is to 'do things', of women to suffer. Even Job was allotted three male comforters to one wife.

Equally, of course, I lay no stress upon so crude a parable as that in the third part of *Henry the Sixth*, where there enters 'a Son that has killed his Father, with the dead body' followed by 'a Father that has killed his Son, with the body in his arms'; and the poor King is given his opportunity to draw the moral of Civil Warfare. You may take these, I say, as two parables against the Wars of the Roses, the loss of that civil balance among the estates which Tudor rule (with all its evident faults) was getting back to a restored equilibrium among ranks and degrees, with the Crown as fulcrum. So in *Troilus*:

> Take but degree away: untune that string,
> And, hark! what discord follows: each thing meets
> In mere oppugnancy...
> And the rude son should strike his father dead.

It is there, in the Folio; but the art of it is primitive, whoever the artist.

To return upon the preponderance of fathers in a

150 PATERNITY IN SHAKESPEARE

Shakespearian playbill.—I propose here to put aside the great mass of those, from the father of Proteus to Polonius, whose stage business is to devise marriages and marriage settlements, pester their offspring with unheeded advice, bully with authority, only to be shown foolish by the event. Antonio, Leonato, Egeus, Baptista, Vincentio—we scarcely remember the names of these 'heavy fathers', to separate them in our minds. They are all positive and mistaken; they all belong to the Plautine tradition and the Plautine stock-in-trade. What is the recipe?—by confession borrowed from Menander, the confession borne out by such fragments of him as survive. *Recipe*, two haggling fathers, a petulant son in love with an undesirable girl, a slave or servant full of makeshifts for the lad—Spice, if you will, with a cook, a termagant wife or a sycophant; mix to taste, and serve, and there you have your dish, from Menander to Calderon and early Molière. When, in Shakespeare, this Plautine business turns tragic, you get the acme of it in the obstinate fatal-foolish strife of old Montague and old Capulet, whose reconciliation Charles Lamb eloquently closes with:

> So did these poor old lords, when it was too late, strive to outgo each other in mutual courtesies.

VIII

Putting these many exorbitant fathers aside, I think you may trace a higher strain of paternal feeling and of correspondent filial affection growing through the Plays, and find that (almost always dominated by the

PATERNITY IN SHAKESPEARE

attraction of youth to youth) it deepens its undertone as Shakespeare goes on. Rosalind legs off to the forest after a good father banished; and takes Celia who, for friendship, leaves a bad father. If in the forest she finds her lover and woos him, to some slight obscuration of that first purpose—well, that is Shakespeare's way.

So, in *The Merchant of Venice*, Portia piously obeys the letter of her father's will, albeit complaining that 'so is the will of a living daughter curbed by the will of a dead father'. But it was all very well, when it comes to the third test, for Nerissa to have talked sophistry about holy men at their death having good inspirations. Her lady knows a trick worth two of that; herself having said that 'the brain may devise laws for the blood, but a hot temper leaps o'er a cold decree; such a hare is madness, the youth, to skip o'er the meshes of good counsel, the cripple'. Wherefore, and having twice escaped against two-to-one odds, rather than lose Bassanio she takes a hand in the game, arranging for minstrelsy and an artless pretty song, innocent of all reference to the occasion. 'Innocent'?—with its suggestive rhyme and chime—'innocent'?—

> Tell me where is fancy *bred*,
> Or in the heart or in the *head*?
> How begot, how nourish*ed*?
> Reply, reply!

—and if you are not quick enough in the uptake to reply that the rhymes lead to 'lead', why, have at you again! It is 'with gazing *fed*'

> And fancy dies
> In the cradle where it lies.

—No; that anagram of 'lead' in the last four letters of 'cradle' is too subtle, perhaps, to be guessed in a moment. But if love's cradle be also his coffin, what were coffins made of but *lead*?

An 'innocent' song? If I may give a Shakespearian twist to a current vulgarism unmeet to be uttered in this company, 'innocent?—Let me not *think*!' Moreover, Bassanio is no fool. In this same play, too, Shylock's long jealous care for his daughter (a certifiable minx) is not to be ignored because, when he finds her fled, his outcry confuses her perfidy with the ducats she has stolen: he has been a most exemplary careful father until she plays him false: and, for a minor point, young Gobbo's play with his blind father has plainly a touch of tenderness. In *All's Well* Helena is shown as worshipping her father's memory, is helped posthumously by his medical skill to win a husband. If, having won him, by her own device she wins his bed—well that again is Shakespeare's way. In drawing your attention to the considerable business of paternity in the Plays I do not suggest that it compares for a moment with the mastery of young love, which is Shakespeare's constant talisman to confront and overpower it even when it wields the authority of Prospero's wand! No small part of the skill in the second scene of *The Tempest*, that marvellous protasis, lies in Miranda's frequent inattention to her father's story. His magic has prepared the hour, drawn the ship to wreck, scattered while preserving her crew and passengers; and now the moment has come to clear his throat and launch on the long apology. But what is Miranda doing? Her eyes, her thoughts, are for the

PATERNITY IN SHAKESPEARE

sea and the vessel that perhaps has carried—she knows not what. 'More to know', of what Prospero starts to tell,

> did never meddle with my thoughts:

and his impatience grows with her inattention.

> Twelve year since, Miranda—twelve year since—
> —Both, both, my girl!

and anon, 'Dost thou attend me?' 'Thou attend'st not' —'Dost thou hear?'... and in the end 'Thou art inclined to sleep'—as later, when the curtain of the cave is drawn, and she looks up from the chess-board to be dazzled at sight of king and courtiers in unspoilt finery, on her exclamation

> O, wonder!
> How many goodly creatures are there here!
> How beauteous mankind is! O brave new world
> That has such people in it!

—'Tis new to *thee*!', answers her father, with an asperity pardonable on the implied slight, disconcerted at the moment on which he was towering alike as parent, majestic person, and mage.

IX

The famous scene of Prince Hal's trying on the crown reaches beyond the ordinary relationship between father and son to touch on that queer antagonism, so often repeated in history, between a reigning monarch and his first-born, his heir apparent. Why this should be, and happen so often, I shall not enquire.

But the two crucial plays in any study of paternity and filial duty in Shakespeare are *Hamlet* and *King Lear*.

Of *Hamlet* I shall say little, being so used in reading that play or seeing it performed—or in the question-begging term, 'interpreted'—to trust the evidence of my own senses as against the refinements of more industrious men, that perhaps to maintain here my belief in the play's magnificent *simplicity* would perhaps receive as little attention as the insistent cry of the child in Hans Andersen's story—'But the Emperor *has* no clothes!' That, out of the tangle of previous attempts, Shakespeare did finally produce (with one ambiguity in the previous relations between Hamlet and Ophelia—and that is none of our business here)—a straightforward tragedy intelligible to anybody, straightly *felt* by anyone in stalls, pit, circle or gallery—of this I am certain now as when in childhood, unaware of such beings as commentators, I first trembled to the play. What is the experimental fact? To this day any travelling company of actors, having played to empty houses, can advertise *Hamlet* with a reasonable prospect of escaping on Friday with their luggage on the proceeds. Can we suppose that Shakespeare, a playwright inviting an audience *and getting it*, and laying, on top of that, its spell upon audiences to this day, produced, as it has been called of late, 'most certainly an artistic failure'? Has the ordinary man taken trouble and paid his money for over three hundred years to see this 'artistic failure'? Can we suppose that he pays to see something 'he cannot understand'? Is that the way of men who make up an audience?

PATERNITY IN SHAKESPEARE

I ask these simple questions because, after long rebellion against much of the criticism that has grown around *Hamlet*, at length I happened on a clearing where someone plainly says the thing that is not. In my youth a gentleman in Philadelphia, U.S.A., had demonstrated that Hamlet was a woman in disguise and in love with Horatio. In my age I find that kind of intelligence still operating. The other day I picked up the programme of a performance at Cambridge with an anthology of criticism including this, by Dr Ernest Jones:

> The main theme is a highly elaborated and disguised account of a boy's love for his mother and correspondent jealousy of, and hatred towards, his father.

By 'father' I assume Dr Jones to mean 'step-father', though the difference is perhaps immaterial to an addict of psycho-analysis, and all 's one to Oedipus! I quote the saw for its helpfulness as an instance of simple perversion. For, of course, to anyone not standing directly upon his head the whole action starts and flows from Hamlet's devotion to his father and his father's memory, disgust at his mother's wedlock (to him incestuous), and the later revelation by his father's ghost of his uncle's crime, with the command of vengeance laid on a gentle soul too sensitive and therefore unequal to it. Why, he, who speaks daggers to his mother, had only to mention his dead father and his language, as Dr Bradley puts it, 'melts into music'.

X

In *Lear* the assertion of *Patria Potestas*, the father's abuse of it, and the sacrifice of Cordelia's loyalty to it with shamefast love, so occupy the meaning of the play that at this time of the argument and the clock I shall offer a crazy suggestion rather than tire you as I might with glimpses at the obvious.

A while ago, in talk with a young man, whom I shall call Adeimantus, because it is not his name, this crazy suggestion leapt up—'Was the Fool in *Lear* Cordelia in disguise?' Pray wait a moment. I admit it to be crazy, shall assert it crazy; yet not so impossible as it looks at first sight. For, consider: Cordelia and the Fool are never on the stage together. There is no Fool to warn Lear of his folly as he commits it, and before his punishment begins. Lear's first mention of him is:

> But where's my fool? I have not seen him this two days.

And a Knight answers:

> Since my young lady's [Cordelia to wit] going into France, the Fool hath much pined him away.

Then later, in Act II, Scene 2, how does Kent, sitting in the stocks and producing a letter, know as he says:

> 'tis from Cordelia,
> Who hath most fortunately been inform'd
> Of my obscured course....

How has he come by this letter? Has it, perhaps, been sleighted to his hand in the cockscomb-cap which the Fool has thrice, on their previous meeting, insisted on his taking? Or again, why that feminine touch when

PATERNITY IN SHAKESPEARE

the Fool, otherwise so plucky, rushes out of the hut at sight of Edgar, screaming?

'No', you will say of course: 'Impossible to think of Cordelia—even in this play so liberal of disguises undetected—as uttering the frank obscenities put into the Fool's mouth!'

Well, and I agree, heartily; but only to offer you a likelier suggestion: which is—that the boy who enacted Cordelia enacted the Fool's part also; that the audience knew this, whether or no the playbill advertised it, and enjoyed the virtuosity of the double performance; that, in short, they were 'in the know'. As Dr Dover Wilson has quite recently reminded us in that concise, illuminating little book—*The Essential Shakespeare*—on which an old comrade may be allowed to congratulate him:

> The whole atmosphere [of an Elizabethan playhouse] must have been extraordinarily intimate and domestic, especially when we remember that the personnel both of the company and of the audience was far more permanent than anything conceivable in modern London. Each member of the cast would be as familiar to the spectators as the individuals of a local football team are to-day to a crowd on the home ground.

Take the hypothesis how you will, it has the merit (I think) of covering the somewhat strange fact that Cordelia and the Fool are never on the stage together; of explaining why, no reason given, the dramatist kicks this most faithful servant out into oblivion and the night, worse requited than 'mine enemy's dog!'

> Though the rain it raineth every day—

on poor fools discarded and left to shiver: finally of providing that audience with a secondary thrill as Lear, staring into the face of his dead daughter, the cord loosened from her neck, recollects the very last fragments of mind and memory and tries to piece them:

> And my—poor fool—is—hanged!

XI

Well, anyhow, *Lear*—to my mind a far greater poem than a play; as, to my mind, a greater play than any *Oedipus* (the two most nearly touching on a point of physical disgust, the putting-out of eyes)—a poem, again to my mind, stretched beyond any theatre's capacity—expresses in the story of the King and his three daughters, of Gloucester and his two sons, the last tear Shakespeare could wring out of fatherhood in authority, of its authority misguided, and the pathetic loyalty of its offspring.

To this I can only offer you, as anticlimax, the testimony of the *Sonnets*, of which the first, easily separated, batch deal with paternity and continuance of a noble name and breed:

> Dear my love, you know
> You had a father; let your son say so.

Thereafter the theme turns, continues, and divagates, into passion between lover and mistress.

I have not, I hope, exaggerated the claim of fatherhood beyond its proper place in Shakespeare. It is there, and quite often acts mischievously: the claim always inferior to that of young love, which persistently defeats it, to reconcile the sins of the parents in the hopes of their children.

XII

To conclude, let me say that I have of purpose omitted from this paper any speculation on Shakespeare's own difference or degree of affection as between his father and his mother. That his father was a sanguine, combative, somewhat ebullient man an accumulation of evidence seems to prove; as to show that his ambition had a theatrical zest, both for himself and for the town of which he was for a period Chief Bailiff. It indicates that he was in his way remarkable, if eccentric; and I have a sense that his son had an affection for him and sometimes used his understanding of this paternal exuberance, playfully, in his comic scenes, without 'giving it away'. But that is mere guess. It may be that John Shakespeare advanced some early ambition by marrying a small heiress of the ancient and gentle family of Arden. But of this Mary Arden, Shakespeare's mother, of what kind of woman or mother she was, we know nothing. For what it is worth, we know that in the quest for coat-armour it was sought at first to impale the fresh coat of Shakespeare with the ancient coat of Arden, and that after an effort or two by the College of Heralds this impalement was given up, and a simple assignment to Shakespeare granted—no why or wherefore as yet ascertained. All that research and weighing of available evidence can do on this point has been done successively by Halliwell Phillipps, Sir Sidney Lee, and (to name no others) last, but not least, by Sir Edmund Chambers. And yet Mary Arden, Shakespeare's mother, remains a ghost to us. She may have been a self-effacing mother, yet exemplary. One would like to believe that she was. But the evidence for this, as for Anne Hathaway's quality as a wife, if not negative, rests on silence, and we will leave it at that. To me it is enough that whoever, and whatever, Shakespeare was, he was of a quality which singles him out among the tribes of men, and is nowise to be accounted for by any domestic or genealogical discovery as yet to hand.

TENNYSON IN 1833

ARTHUR HENRY HALLAM died in Vienna of a sudden lesion of the brain on September 15, 1833. He had not completed his twenty-third year. Comparing what he achieved in that small span (a volume of his *Remains* appeared in 1834) with the laments of all who knew him over a promise untimely blasted, one has to go back even to Sir Philip Sidney, perhaps forward to Rupert Brooke, to find a like English echo of the *Tu Marcellus eris*. To be sure the other two were granted time to achieve more, to do one or two perfect things; but of neither does the actual accomplishment quite outweigh the assurance, the passionate agreement, among all who mourned over Arthur Hallam that a bright, particular day-star had shot down and been quenched.

The assurance was passionate in that these friends (mostly of Cambridge) lamented him not only for his intellectual promise but for a sweetness of disposition which can best be understood by reading over stanzas CIX–CXIII of *In Memoriam*.

They were a distinguished band, too; not at all of the sort to be taken in by flashiness or empty pretence, whether of head or heart—James Spedding the judicious, W. H. Thompson the fastidious (afterwards Master of Trinity), Trench (afterwards Archbishop of Dublin), Alford (afterwards Dean of Canterbury), Blakesley (afterwards Dean of Lincoln), Merivale (afterwards Dean of Ely), Richard Monckton Milnes, J. M. Kemble, Douglas Heath (Senior Wrangler in 1832), Charles Buller, Stephen Spring Rice, the Lushingtons and, foremost and dearest of all, Alfred Tennyson. Many years later, in 1866, Milnes (who had become Lord Houghton), at the re-housing of the Cambridge Union in its new quarters, could fairly claim: 'I am inclined to believe that the members of that generation were, for the wealth of their promise, a rare body of men such as this University has seldom contained'. But, lest their *desiderium* for Hallam, or any tinge in it, be set down to tribal partiality, let us hear an Oxford man—and no small one at that—Mr Gladstone:

> It would be easy to show what in the varied forms of human excellence he might, had life been granted him, have accomplished; much more difficult to point a finger and to say, 'This he could never have done'.

Certainly this group of Cambridge men had, one and all, a great capacity for friendship. And it may be remembered, by the way, that as (for their varied talents) the world began to take account of them so their common enthusiasm greatly eased Tennyson's early steps to fame; he, for his part, sitting and playing the recluse somewhat ostentatiously in a 'den'; dressing carelessly, smoking tobacco largely, and in that state of life now and then throwing off such mighty-petty condescensions as 'Vex not thou the poet's mind With thy shallow wit',..'Dark-browed sophist, come not near', etc.

But there is evidence enough even without *In Memoriam* that the friendship which knit Alfred Tennyson with Arthur Hallam—'more than my brothers are to me'—was singular among these others, passing the love of woman. It had been deepened and, as it were, sanctified by Hallam's engagement to Tennyson's sister, Emily: their wedding-day fixed when the blow fell. The very belatedness of *In Memoriam*—which waited some seventeen years upon it—speaks of that blow's sudden ruin of domestic hope. It stunned: and if we mark the slowness of the recovery, we do it at this distance of time with no intrusion upon a private grief which Tennyson himself in time revealed, to reconcile it with such mourning as we all sooner or later share, but simply because he was a great poet; because great poets pass into the world's property; and the world, whether they like it or not, will insist on trying to explain them by circumstance and their private lives—as though the ultimate secret could be found there! The limit of right, if pathetic, curiosity to discover 'how the thing was done' may easily be overstepped into impertinence (as it has been in some recent attempts to account for Wordsworth); but the authors of *The Prelude* and *In Memoriam* courted the risk, and with Tennyson the risk was little enough. We know of him—who risked more contradiction in saying it of the Duke of Wellington—that whatever record leap to light he never shall be shamed.

The blow of Hallam's death, then, stunned him for a while into disheartened silence; but not that blow alone. The volume of *Poems by Alfred Tennyson*, misdated 1833 on its title page, had in fact appeared before Christmas, 1832; and in April, 1833, the *Quarterly Review* came out with a would-be scathing critique—a deplorable performance. It starts (as people in the wrong are the slowest to forgive) with a little carry-over of spite from the *Quarterly's* too famous attack of 1818 on *Endymion* and 'Mr Keats (if that be his real name, for we almost doubt that any man in his senses would put his real name to such a rhapsody)'—'What *are* Keats?' in other words—promising now to introduce 'to the admiration of our more sequestered readers a new prodigy of genius—another and a brighter star of that galaxy or *milky way* of poetry of which the lamented Keats was the harbinger'. There is no need here to pursue the reviewer, who now and then deviates into just reproof, through the schoolboy flippancies with which he pelts Tennyson. 'The Lady of Shalott was, it seems, a spinster who had, under some unnamed penalty, a certain web to weave'—Here the man's cleverness and his omniscience fail him together: he might have guessed, though he did not know, that the poem was founded on a legend—actually an Italian story, *Donna di Scalotta*. As for *The Miller's Daughter*: 'Millers' daughters, poor things, have been so generally betrayed by their sweethearts, that it is refreshing to find that Mr Tennyson has united himself to *his* miller's daughter in lawful wedlock'. That is the sort of stuff, and is as easy as falling off a stool. But this was the *Quarterly Review*, with all the *Quarterly's* heavy prestige; and the effect of it on Tennyson, attested by many letters in his son's *Life*, is hinted at by himself in that poem of his old age, *Merlin and The Gleam*

> Once at the croak of a Raven
> who crost it,
> A barbarous people,

> Blind to the magic,
> And deaf to the melody,
> Snarl'd at and cursed me.
> A demon vext me,
> The light retreated,
> The landskip darken'd,
> The melody deaden'd,
> The Master whisper'd
> 'Follow The Gleam'.

Beyond doubt Tennyson was abnormally sensitive, even for a poet, under attack. Twice only, we believe, he publicly forgot his own juvenile advice to 'let them rave', and retorted in print; the first time on Wilson, 'Crusty Christopher', the second on Lytton-Bulwer for criticising (in 1847) his acceptance of a pension. For the first retort he apologised in a private letter; the second he regretted and would not republish. In 1833 he crept away with his wound, buried himself like the hero in *Maud*, with a smoke-screen of tobacco for extra cover. 'I am black-blooded like all the Tennysons', his son quotes him as saying: 'I remember all the malignant things said against me, but little of the praise'.

He had as yet but little of praise (save his friends') to cheer him; small fame; next to nothing of popularity. The day of Scott, Byron, Moore, when poetry commanded huge sales and high prices, was over. Tennyson as a beginner had received £11 for the 1830 volume, and as late as 1842 (over the two volumes published in that year) he could still find matter for exulting that '500 of my books are sold: according to Moxon's brother I have made a sensation!' It may be that men's appetite for poetry fails in the exhaustion of a long war.

To-day the literary reviews, to their credit, give it (as it seems to us) fair encouragement, which brings no proportionate gain to poet or publisher. Still, they are fair to the extent that they deal or try to deal mostly with it on its own merits, as poetry: whereas for a whole generation after Waterloo political (and therefore adventitious) prejudice infected pure criticism in England, and for three reviewers in any four it was enough that a young aspirant had been patted on the head by poor Leigh Hunt: he would at once be 'Johnny' or 'Alfred', and treated accordingly. At any rate, and from whatever causes, through a long interval before 1832 English poetry lay in the doldrums. Byron had died while Tennyson was in his teens, Keats and Shelley preceding him. Southey continued to write epics, and Landor to chisel verse which few regarded. Wordsworth and Coleridge lasted on, venerated ruins; and there was no obvious inheritor of the laureateship when Wordsworth should come to die. It must go to the credit of American discernment that recognition came quicker to him yonder than at home. As Mrs Brotherton, his friend and neighbour in later life, has recorded:

> Honour to whom honour is due. While England had as yet given her new poet but a hesitating welcome America received his 1833 volume with open arms. The younger and more impulsive nation had been at once fascinated, and Tennyson's poetry was already in the hearts and on the lips of the best Americans while it was being damned with faint praise by the great majority of his own countrymen.

The law of copyright—or, rather, the absence of it—

precluded a more solid tribute. But kind hearts are more than royalties.

It is hard, at a hundred years' remove, to understand why his own country, so sorely in need of a new poet, was so slow in the uptake. It would be harder if we had not recently passed through a period of revolt against him and wondered at its brief excesses. Clearly he belonged to the Coleridge-Wordsworth-Keats-Shelley tradition. They had been the younger gods to him and his intimates at Cambridge; and without these forerunners Tennyson—the Tennyson that we know—would never have been. A well-organised persecution can often be far more effective than we, as a tolerant nation, are disposed to realise; and the haters of the 'Cockney School', as they called it, were a compact body, if sterile. But as clearly Tennyson, though he derived from tradition, belonged to no 'school', but was a man of his own hands. Affection had not blinded Arthur Hallam—it had over-stimulated, rather, his optic nerve—when, reviewing the small 1830 volume in the *Englishman's Magazine*, he roundly declared:

The author imitates no one: we recognise the spirit of his age, but not the individual form of this or that writer. His thoughts bear no more resemblance to Byron or Scott, Shelley or Coleridge, than to Homer or Calderon, Firdusi or Calidara. We have remarked five distinctive excellences in his own manner....

Of course Tennyson was never, even in youth, original as all *that*. But markedly individual he was, and eminently original he was felt to be by young men growing up to poetry—by Aubrey Vere for instance:
—and about that originality there was for us a wild inexplicable

magic and a deep pathos, though hardly as simple as Wordsworth's pathos, and with nothing of its homeliness; and the character of his language was nearly the opposite of that which Wordsworth had, at least in his youth, asserted to be the true poetic diction—viz., the language of common life among the educated....

We may have to say a word on this before concluding.

Day after day my sister and I used to read them [the 1832 poems] as we drove up and down the 'close green ways' of our woods. Our pony soon detected our abstracted mood. Several times he nearly upset us down a bank.... We sometimes sketched an imaginary likeness of the unknown poet. We determined that he must be singularly unlike Shelley; that his step must be not rapid but vague, that there would be on his face less of light but more of dream; that his eye would be that of one who saw little where the many see much, and saw much where the many see little. Wholly unlike the young poet must be the countenance of him who had long been the chief object of our poetic veneration, the great contemplative Bard—Coleridge.

Thus eagerly did imaginative youth, impressionable while naturally refined, fasten upon that which the reviewers had overlooked, the *permanent* in Tennyson.

But Tennyson,

> as the snail, whose tender horns being hit,
> Shrinks backward in his shelly cave with pain,
> And there all smother'd up in shade doth sit,

withdrew with his sorrow and his hurt to an attic. For ten years the world saw nothing of him, his old friends little; and he wrote few letters. 'In letters', he said, 'words too often prove a bar of hindrance instead of a bond of union.' That was his mood: and 'my friends have long since ceased to write, knowing me to be so irregular a correspondent'.

But this hermit life meant neither laziness nor merely the sulks; but a long and hard course of self-discipline through which the man born a poet taught himself to become an exquisite artist as well. Looking back on 1833–42 we can see this period of solitude and perseverance in defeat as the noblest in his career; morally out-valuing even its great ultimate reward. He began, it would seem, by falling to work upon his former poems: revising, condensing, cutting, polishing, until some of them reappeared in 1842 as scarcely the same things. This labour of the file is notoriously tricky work, and with some poets—Burns, for example—often disastrous. To change the image, some wines depend on the first runnings from the vat, their native virtue left to ferment and mature of themselves, without 'doctoring'. But Tennyson's first outpourings, many of them, needed clarifying: and his judgment in this operation was usually sound, though not always. Rightly enough, for instance, he cut out such things as *The Darling Room*, and by chastening immensely improved *The Lady of Shalott*. On the other hand we agree with FitzGerald that he largely spoiled *The Miller's Daughter* by alterations, probably due, if we could trace them back, to the *Quarterly's* ridicule. The critic had shied at '*gummy* chestnut-buds'. To learn of an enemy is good counsel; but what are chestnut-buds if not gummy?—it should be their Homeric epithet. The revised version advanced them a fortnight and made them hang 'in masses thick with milky cones'. The meal on the miller's face offended likewise and was wiped off, to FitzGerald's regret, and ours:

> I met in all the close green ways,
>   While walking with my rod and line,
> The miller with his mealy face
>   And long'd to take his hand in mine.

So it stood originally, and was altered for the worse to—

> I met in all the close green ways,
>   While walking with my line and rod,
> The wealthy miller's mealy face
>   Like the moon in an ivytod.

The critic pounced upon that, of course. "'Line and rod" a metonym for "rod and line"!' But the meal was what choked him—

> The very air about the door
>   Made misty with the floating meal!

Meal in a mill! 'God shield us! a lion among ladies....' So out went all mention of meal. But we regret more the excision of one simple Wordsworthian stanza:

> Remember you the clear moonlight
>   That whiten'd all the eastern ridge,
> When o'er the water dancing white
>   I stepp'd upon the old mill bridge?
> I heard you whisper from above,
>   A lute-toned whisper, 'I am here'.
> I murmur'd 'Speak again, my love,
>   The stream is loud; I cannot hear'.

One could wish he had preferred to excise *The May Queen* with its sequels. But the sobering effect of Wordsworth, as silent admonisher, sometimes even as model, upon a genius so unlike Wordsworth's is evident

TENNYSON IN 1833

throughout those years of discipline. Now and again, as might be expected of a disciple engaged in correcting his own natural bent for diction, Tennyson strives for simplicity to fall into *simplesse*, even into bathos:

> An hour had passed—and sitting straight
> Within the low-wheeled chaise,
> Her mother trundled to the gate
> Behind the dappled grays.

—like Mrs John Gilpin, in all but her qualms. Now and again, whether in self-distrust or obedience, avoiding excess, he cuts out a fine stanza or, over part of it, lets pass a line too pompous for its meaning—

> I read before my eyelids dropt their shade—

which is, in a different way, 'poetic diction' as flagrant as that against which Coleridge and Wordsworth had revolted.

It is not, however, by several lines, stanzas, or even poems, that Tennyson's hard apprenticeship should be judged; nor yet by the success of the Wordsworthian idylls which opened the second volume of *Poems by Alfred Tennyson* in 1842, though Wordsworth so far relaxed his habitual parcimoniousness in praising others as to say: 'Mr Tennyson, I have been endeavouring all my life to write a pastoral like your *Dora* and have not succeeded'. Others have condemned these and other idylls as Alexandrine—which actually is no condemnation at all. (Theocritus himself, father of the mode, wrote in Alexandria, and maybe invented it there.) It seems more pertinent to point out (if we are right in detecting it) that in the two 1842 volumes a

great part of the first was corrected, and of the second composed, 'against the grain': that precisely through this hard chiselling on reluctant material Tennyson's hand acquired its amazing artistry: and, for evidence, that later, when success had come and he allowed himself in *Enoch Arden* to indulge his bent for decorative over-writing, a plain tale gets caught (as Bagehot notes) amid 'ocean-smelling osiers', 'long convolvuluses', and is
strangled with (its) waste fertility.

But, to our thinking, the most evident triumph of the strong will at work appeared after seventeen years, and appropriately enough in the monument built of the sorrow that had almost caused despair. A notebook containing the earliest manuscript of *The Two Voices*—a poem written while Tennyson 'longed for death', as he confessed—contains on a stray sheet the section of *In Memoriam* beginning with 'Fair ship that from the Italian shore': and in later pages four other sections, two of them divided by the first draft of *Morte d'Arthur*. Already upon the mountains of Gilboa the dews were gathering. For the ultimate 'fields of offering', let any student of poetry, and of the Elegy in particular, in whatever land written or in whatever age, putting aside fashion as well as he can, consider *In Memoriam*. Where will he find another lament at once so passionate and so marmoreal, which also shows that blending of private mourning for a young man whose promise all but a few intimates had forgotten with the universal grief attendant on human life? Then let him consider the mere and magnificent technique by which—through subtle choice and use of metre, through breaks and sections—his *interest* is sustained through an elegy of almost epic length; and he must at once admire the achievement and revere the courage of the man who, a hundred years ago, took up the ruins of his life and of them erected a nobler self—and a masterpiece.

WILLIAM BARNES

I

WILLIAM BARNES was born in the first year of the last century and died in 1886, the year before Queen Victoria's first jubilee. The story of his long life may be told in a very few sentences. His father tilled a farm in the beautiful Vale of Blackmore, in Dorset; and the boy grew up among the labourers of that still-unspoilt land; but his parents, on the schoolmaster's report that he was 'quick at his books', articled him, at 17, to an attorney in Dorchester. After some five years of this employ he threw it up to teach in a school over the Wiltshire border. Its success encouraged him after two years to remove the school to Dorchester. For some time he had amused his leisure with writing verse, attempting woodcuts in the manner of Bewick, and improving himself with passion in the science of philology, at that time mewing its mighty youth.

In that year, 1838, or thereabouts, Barnes, having taken Holy Orders, entered St John's, Cambridge, as a 'ten years' man'. Now I suppose it unlikely that any of you, my hearers, have ever met with a 'ten years' man' or would know one if you met him. But that again is almost humanly impossible, since the race finally expired under statute in 1860. But a 'ten years' man' was one in priest's orders who came up from the country and could distribute his period of residence over ten years while qualifying for a B.D. May I add that St John's grew an astounding crop of them (in one year the College Books confess to seventy-eight) in its intelligible if less than saintly desire to keep its hold on the Lady Margaret Chair of Divinity, the electorate to which was confined to B.D.'s and D.D.'s, 'dispersed throughout the world'.

Barnes took his B.D. in 1850, being by this time pastor of Whitcombe in the Isle of Wight, a post which he held until his translation back to Dorset in 1862 as Rector of Came where he ministered until his death in 1886. It is here that I invite you to be introduced to him and his surroundings.

II

In the 'seventies or early 'eighties of the last century a visitor who had made his way to the village of Winterborne Came in Dorset, about a mile-and-a-half from Dorchester, having run it down in its nest of elms amid the nine or ten Winterbornes or Winterbournes—Winterborne Abbas, Winterborne Came, Winterbourne Earl's, Winterbourne Gunner, Winterbourne Monkton, Winterbourne Stoke—that cluster in Dorset and Wilts, would have found welcome under the low verandah of its Rectory, with cider or ale, tobacco and hospitable talk in its shade. The house—straw-thatched, rioted over by creepers—was set around with trees. Swallows populated its eaves; bees hummed in its garden.... I am painting you (however you suspect it) no nook of fancy, but the residence of an actual man, whom you will find at once idyllic—shrewd and solid.

He is just past eighty, but hale yet, white-bearded with an aspect which suggests what you can recollect of St Mark's from any number of stained-glass windows. His hair, too, is white, and he wears it patriarchally long, that it touches his shoulders. He is dressed in a long black coat, knee-breeches, black stockings, stout buckled shoes. He has a rustic pair of shoulders with a scholar's stoop; and his tunable voice, after greeting, will continue in the accent of educated English or slide into broad Doric unconsciously as he admits you to intimacy.

Let me continue for a while with the 'historic present'. You will be made welcome within the Rectory, the down-stair living rooms of which consist of a dark little dining-room, lined with books; a brighter parlour, a trifle overcrowded with 'works of art'—some of home-manufacture, others picked up by the Rector on his rare peregrinations, long since forsworn; last, a small 'study', in which he shuts himself up of an evening, only to be tempted forth when his two daughters close the day with music and voice in the outer room. These are his 'blest pair of Sirens' (at what cost of self-abnegation patriarchally taken for granted in those days we must not enquire). Between them they manage the choir of their father's primitive small Church, a quarter of a mile away, which contains (as he will point out) two objects of interest—a wonderful screen, and an autograph of Napoleon III who, as Prince Napoleon, had somehow attended a marriage here and signed the register. A far cry from Winterborne Came to the Tuileries and Sedan!

III

The date of my imaginary visit is (you will suppose) the summer of 1882, and the visit itself a sort of pilgrimage: the pilgrim (if you can put yourself in his place, Gentlemen), a very young man, moderately shy but emboldened by hero-worship: too callow as yet to have learnt that, among the remarkable works of God, on personal acquaintance a poet is apt to be the most disappointing. But this one is not. You admit with a blush the motive that brought you: and that, strange to say, does not offend him. As Matthew Arnold once remarked of a stranger who hailed him for a major poet, 'Of course, I didn't believe a word of it—yet the assurance was undeniably gratifying'. Nor is the Rector offended again by the confession that you are killing two birds with one stone, so to speak; that you have been piously tramping, exploring 'the Hardy Country' —as it has since come to be called—and for yourself identifying scenes since identified and mapped in handbooks. The Rector plunges at once into that broad Doric towards which he has been gradually slipping from courtesy to something like intimacy. 'Oh, yes! He has known Tom Hardy since he was *so* high.' But, unlike most people who have known somebody since he was *so* high, he believes Tom Hardy to be a genius: goes into details of Hardy's family upbringing, his marriage, his prospects—worldly prospects, that is. 'Novel-writing', the Rector opines, 'must be a hazardous vocation': and you infer from his tone about it rather than from any actual words that he inclines to class it with dancing or singing in Opera, as something that with luck can command large sums but lives at the mercy of popular favour, is 'a stuff will not endure' for a livelihood, carries in itself the seed of Time's destruction as surely as does a prima donna's vocal chord. Also your host knows nothing of any 'Reading Public'. He has never had one: and you are disposed to guess that he is disposed to doubt if reading be altogether good for the public—novel-reading in particular. He was born in 1801. So you see that your host's concern with Thomas Hardy's prospects considerably differs from that which I may presume to be yours.

Anxieties over Hardy's *artistic* development as a novelist, one perceives, do not concern your host—do not even occur to him. Though Fielding and Scott, Jane Austen, Peacock, Dickens, Disraeli, Thackeray, Trollope, have written—though he reads French with ease and is acquainted with Balzac—still, a novel is, well, the sort of thing Lydia Languish's maid still brings home in a basket from the Circulating Library. On the other hand, the hundred years that have failed to eradicate this superstition, have been quite as powerless against the beliefs rooted in literate men (a million times cheated and upon the millionth proved true) that a man has only to capture and pin down in verse one thought or emotion about God or a blackbird or Amaryllis or what-not and it will outlast marble or bronze; preserving the transient rose—

> Past ruin'd Ilion Helen lives,
>   Alcestis rises from the shades:
> Verse calls them forth; 'tis verse that gives
>   Immortal youth to mortal maids;

—and the mischief is that once now and again the verse-makers do it.

> Dead is Augustus, Maro is alive....

IV

Even so light a singer as Herrick found himself able to prophesy blithely—

> Trust in good verses then;
> They only will aspire
> When pyramids, as men,
> Are lost i' th' funeral fire.
>
> And when all bodies meet
> In Lethe to be drown'd
> Then only numbers sweet
> With endless life are crown'd.

So this other old West-country parson—who also has sung 'of Brooks, of Blossomes, Birds, and Bowers', as also 'of Maypoles, Hock-carts, Wassails, Wakes' or their nineteenth-century equivalents in parish walkings, bridals, boxing-bouts, harvest home suppers, dances in the barn—has little doubt of the permanence of his lays, although (as we shall see) he has done almost everything humanly possible to discourage their being read by anybody. He is quite cheerful and assured about this, however. For have not Tennyson and Palgrave praised them and made room for them in *The Golden Treasury*? And truly what contemporary certificate could be higher? Remember not only what *The Golden Treasury* includes, but the place and moment when this or that poem opened a sudden vista or surmise of poetry—remember even how the awakening words lie upon the page.

So our old Rector, admitting you to intimacy, has presently no reluctance over reading a specimen or two of his own in his native Doric. For example this, entitled *Children's Children*—

>Oh! if my ling'ren life should run
> Through years a-reckon'd ten by ten,
>Below the never-tirin' Sun,
> Till beabes agean be wives an' men;
>An' stillest deafness should ha' bound
>My ears at last vrom ev'ry sound;
>Though still my eyes in that sweet light
>Should have the sight o' sky an' ground;
> Would then my steate
> In time so leate,
>Be jay or pain, be pain or jay?
>
>When Zunday then, a'weanen dim
> As thease that now's a'cloosen still,
>Mid lose the zun's down-zinken rim
> In light behind the vire-bound hill:
>An' when the bells' last peal's a-rung,
>An' I mid zee the wold an' young
>A-vlocken by, but shoulden hear,
>However near, a voot or tongue:
> Mid such a zight
> In that soft light
>Be jay or pain, be pain or jay?
>
>If I should zee among em all,
> In merry youth a-gilden by,
>My son's bwold son, a-grown man-tall,
> Or daughter's daughter, woman-high;
>An' she mid smile wi' your good feace,
>Or she might walk your comely peace,

WILLIAM BARNES

But seem, although a-chatten loud,
So still's a cloud, in that bright please;
Would youth so feair
A-passen there
Be jay or pain, be pain or jay?

V

Let me take these verses—a fair sample of Barnes at his most characteristic and almost at his best with the refrain—of which he was over-fond—better handled, technically, than usual—as a text for some observations.

To begin with, I claim them to be genuine poetry. They are musical (if you demur to this, Gentlemen, lay the fault upon me, bred to a more westerly and less Saxon dialect. They make music, at any rate, and when their 'fair course is not hindered', in the mind's ear). And their music weds itself to that 'emotion recollected in tranquillity' which is the test of a meditative lyric. To pronounce their thought commonplace carries no necessary condemnation, since most of the best lyrics in the world have been emotional expressions of a commonplace—the frailty of fame, the rapture of love, the end of ambition, the transience of the rose: and Johnson had the right of it in censuring Cowley for failure to observe 'by what means the ancients have continued to delight through all the changes of human manners'. I am aware that a number of our younger poets and critics dispute this and incline rather, while they reject Browning as difficult in the wrong way, to appraise remoteness of subject, subtlety of search in form and emotion, with a consequent strain on the reader, as among the higher, even the necessary, virtues of verse. Well, Time will bring their theory and their practice to the test, and who is the lover of Poetry but should wish well to experiments and dogmatics which, even by their vehemence in rejecting old lamps for new, are proving Poetry itself immortal and keeping the instinct for it re-animated. The older religions may put up their shutters one by one, but the trade of the Muses goes on.

And so, avoiding controversy, I would point out that the verses quoted treat of something a little beyond a commonplace. It is a commonplace, to be sure, observable in daily life, that our neighbours who suffer from blindness are far more patient under their affliction, though to most of us it would seem the heavier, than are the deaf under theirs; are less morose about it, less given to accuse their fate or to shift the annoyance upon their fellows. And Barnes here touches (as I think most gently) on that deafness of the dead, supposed with helpless ache to communicate, which not a few have anticipated in terror as less tolerable than eternal blindness. 'It all rests on fallacy'—But does it? Bethink you there is a truth of emotion as well as a truth of fact, the one at least as necessary to poetry as the other. Indeed in poetry—as in our own better moments (if I may use that term without smugness)—moments, I mean, when—

> We feel that we are greater than we know,

to separate them were an attempt of folly, the emotional surmise being every whit as much a fact as the grave itself. Yes, and I dare say that even as a physical fact the tone of one familiar voice, or the murmur of many, will follow the dying consciousness down beyond vision of any face.

> For who, to *dumb* forgetfulness a prey,
> This pleasing *anxious* being ere resign'd?...

And further I would point it out as an idiosyncrasy that, susceptible as Barnes' vision is to the panorama of the countryside, and true to it at any point of description, whenever he touches lea, meadow or hanging wood with their particular inhabitants of tree or flower, his eye is more *general* (so to say) than his ear, being rather preoccupied with the men, women, children moving upon the scene than with the discriminations between this or that flower or weed for which John Clare finds his subtle epithets. Barnes, as a rural poet, stands nearer to Robert Bloomfield in this. To both the rural background subserves the labouring lives that move upon it and belong, with their ploughings, to their harvest-homes; while Barnes sees a deeper, memorial purport in the background and in *his* 'field full of folk'; is more attentive, as more sensitive, to the bodies, dear *because* transitory, that labour and earn lease of this green life between a shade and a shade; specially to their *voices*. And why specially to their voices is a question I must next 'attempt'.

VI

Barnes chooses to write in dialect. Now a poet who uses dialect is at once supposed—even by critics who should know better—to be challenging comparison with Burns: and if his name happen to be Barnes, the temptation would seem to be irresistible. Let me accept that foolishness just so far as it serves to illustrate by way of contrast the material, the vocabulary, the technique of that other and greater poet who also wrote of rural life and in dialect. Please understand that I shall not be comparing their real and ultimate values *as poets*. For speaking roughly let it be granted as obvious that Burns must always stand above Barnes's competition. He has so many more strings to his lyre, and so many of these deeper. They range from *Mary Morison* and *Tam o' Shanter* down to such vulgarities as 'A man's a man for a' that'. But there is the range, the scope; and these must count.

Now we all know, or have been told often enough, how Burns took the old songs of Ayrshire, sang them over to himself on his walks or at his ploughing, took a line or a refrain of it, wove a new lyric as imperishable and apparently spontaneous as the song of a lark. That was the way of Burns's genius; but it was an artistic process, not wholly unconscious. But to take 'Ye banks and braes', for example, as an unpremeditated gush of heart to the head—or, for that matter, of brains to the head—is to ignore the process.

And so with Barnes in *his* way. When a genuine countryman writes genuine poetry to genuine dialect, there is always a disposition in the critic to talk of 'woodnotes wild', profuse, unpremeditated outpourings, 'direct exhalations of the soil', that sort of thing. But if Barnes's emotional inspiration be here and there a thought too sentimental for the taste of to-day, in his

WILLIAM BARNES

technique there is no gush at all. Every page of him, rather, betrays a careful and scholarly polish such as you detected, no doubt, in the verses I read just now with their internal chime—

> An' when the bells' last peal's a-rung,
> An' I mid zee the wold an' young
> A-vlocken by, but shoulden *hear*,
> However *near*, a voot or tongue....

—while even when one meets with a gap in the structure or a wayward rhyme the chances are that the poet knows about it and is deliberately concealing art with art. As Thomas Hardy noted of him, he 'really belonged to the literary school of such poets as Tennyson, Gray and Collins, rather than to that of the old unpremeditated singers in dialect'. Primarily spontaneous, he was academic closely after; and we find him warbling his native wood-notes with a watchful eye on the pre-determined score; a far remove from the popular impression of him as the naïve and rude bard who sings only because he must, and who submits the uncouth lines of his page to us without knowing how they came there! Thus far Hardy and he might have added, 'If you blame this method in Barnes, what about Theocritus?'

VII

But now, concerning this dialect—

Some years ago a few words of mine in praise of Barnes drew a surprise attack from Andrew Lang, who of course ran up Burns as his great gun. Now Lang was no vulgar disputant, to mislead his readers into supposing that I had exalted Barnes against Burns as a poet: but after dismissing my man's poetical pretensions ('if any' as they say in Whitehall) with cavalier ease, he took the ground that Scots was a *language* whereas Dorset was but a debased dialect of English.

Now that Scots is a language nobody denies (who has heard it), or that it has been used by a line of eminent 'makers' for centuries and, as it were, consecrated by that use. But that Dorset was, or is, a debased dialect of English Barnes had spent a long life in disproving: and Barnes was a learned and acute philologer (of his period, be it understood) with a library well stocked in all languages, especially the Teutonic and Scandinavian; was a classic moreover, who read with pupils for the Indian Civil Service, not without success, and had considerable skill in the Mediterranean tongues. So here was a knowledgeable scholar, a painstaking glossarian, who allowed—indeed proclaimed on his title-pages—'Dorset' to be a dialect, but would have maintained against any man that it is so in the exact sense in which Burns's 'Ayrshire' is a dialect of Scots. Let me quote his own words for this, printed in 'A Dissertation on the Dorset Dialect' prefixed to his *Poems of Rural Life*, second edition with enlarged glossary, published as early as 1847—

The Dorset dialect is a broad and bold shape of the English language, as the Doric was of the Greek. It is rich in humour, strong in raillery and hyperbole; and altogether as fit a vehicle of rustic feeling and thought as the Doric is found in the *Idylls* of Theocritus. Some people who may have been taught to consider it as having originated from corruption of the written

English, may not be prepared to hear that it is not only a separate offspring from the Anglo-Saxon tongue, but purer, and in some cases richer, than the dialect which is chosen as the national speech: purer inasmuch as it retains many words of Saxon origin for which the English substitutes echoes of Latin, Greek or French derivation; and richer, inasmuch as it has distinctive words for many things which book-English can hardly distinguish but by periphrasis.

—instancing, to support his case, several single and particular words into which a Dorsetshire labourer would divide what we clumsily call a *root*. A *mock*, for example, is the stump just above the root, a *moot* is the underground part of a felled tree, a *strawen* a set of colonists thrown up by the parent root as it spreads, a *wride* an issue or cluster of sprouts from any lopped stump above ground. Well, we are losing (be it granted) these nice distinctions: but they all came in with the use of man in his generations and successive perfectibilities for his job. Barnes in his glossary has a dozen terms or so for the various parts of a hay-waggon. They are older, but are they therefore 'purer', than the names (which *must* be invented, after all) for the intricate new parts of a flying machine? And as for the claim 'richer'—good Heavens, Gentlemen, where would our language be now, or our literature, but for their power to assimilate new words for new things?

But there you have Barnes's life-long and passionate contention for the Dorset speech: that it was the lingering relic of pure West Saxon; that it had not only preserved its purity, but had in the slow growth of ages perfected itself to all moral needs, and that it was dead or dying, passing with *him*. And that, Gentlemen—if my own observation may suggest it—is the secular fallacy of all archaeologists, specially of philologers; and, by a sort of mental somersault, even more specially of men and women vowed and banded to preserve the King's English. The older folk of Dorset (he held) drew in the true phonetic with their mothers' milk; to revivify it, the local bees had swarmed their last about his own cradle. The dialect (says Barnes) in which he, the author, writes 'is spoken in its greatest purity in the secluded and beautiful Vale of Blackmore. He need not observe that in the towns the poor commonly speak a mixed jargon, violating the canons of the pure dialect, as well as those of English'.

VIII

Nevertheless, and allowing this, I cannot see reason for turning any one dialect of English into a sort of Yellowstone Park. It is unfair to dwellers in the selected district and handicaps those who escape from it. And why, as farmer and labourer are at this moment paid, should they not seek escape? For my own part, supposing myself for the moment a benevolent despot (God forbid!), I should decree that every boy and girl in the land, gentle and simple, were brought up to speak English bi-lingually: that is, conversant with their native dialect in which they could meet on neighbourly footing, conversant also with that schooled English which after all is the standard for educated men and women in daily life—with a difference of course when we try to write it, in prose, and with a still greater difference when we try to write it in verse. But always, whether in prose or in verse, our best literature thrives by being fed from above and below—if you like it, from rain and manure. Try to bethink you what our literature would have been if any dictator could have pronounced on the paragon Chaucer, 'this is the limit'.

But that is the too common mistake with antiquarian philologers. Change and decay in all around they see, but perceive not that, as their own gardens might teach them, change and decay are conditions of organic growth.

To be sure the change, the decay, must have their natural healthy limits, and many will echo Barnes's lament that—

> As increasing communication among the inhabitants of different parts of England, and the spread of school-education among the lower ranks of our population, tend to substitute book-English for the provincial dialects, it is likely that, after a few years, many of them will linger only in the more secluded parts of the land, if they live at all....

Well, I suppose that while most of us cherish, as we look back, a deep affection for this or that schoolmaster, its depth is usually commensurate with his unlikeness to others of his vocation; that, for some reason, few love them in the aggregate. The like may be affirmed, perhaps, of motorists. But these both are broadly disseminating this communication among the inhabitants of different parts of England, with 'wireless' and 'loud speakers' and the 'talkies' to help. In my own opinion, Gentlemen, far too much of this change is laid at the Schoolmaster's door: far too little to bad agricultural policy, draining our countryside into the towns by higher wages for less-skilled work, and concomitantly by the breaking up of the old land-owning class by taxation and the letting loose on their acres of city-men—loan-mongers as old Cobbett called them in his post-war day a century ago—usurers with their week-end guests for tennis and bridge.

IX

If you ask, 'What is to be done about it?' I can only answer here that, the ruin admitted, a more unpractical way of preserving the *poetry* of his countryside could hardly be invented than that which Barnes employed. No more than Burns does he, poetically, ever patronise his rustics. In his heart he is one of them, he shares their simplest emotions and weaves these to his tune. But when the tune has to be set down on paper he transfers it into hieroglyphics which in themselves imply a scholar's patronage. For if his verse be addressed to his happy rustics, how can such possibly deal with his intricate phonetic signs—accents, diaereses, digammas, thetas, to distinguish 'th' from 'dh' and what-not? Moreover, even for scholars, these phonetic signs can never, in my experience, convey the exact pronunciation to any ear. It has been said of my own part of the world that the parish of any one of twelve jurymen could be told by the way in which he 'kissed the book'. We must surely suppose that if a man write poetry he desires to communicate. If he write it for a little clan he should set it down in a form that clan can grasp; and if he seek a wider audience, again he spoils his

WILLIAM BARNES

chance by using a queer invented notation for which (to speak bluntly) the reader has no time.

X

And yet, strained out of pedantic disguises, the residuum of Barnes is pure poetry not to be missed by a clean palate. When Andrew Lang slighted the worth of it, I contented myself with copying down a verse or two, unknown to him, and sending them—from a poem, *The Wife a-Lost*:

> Since I noo mwore do zee your feace,
>   Up steairs or down below,
> I'll zit me in the lwonesome pleace
>   Where flat-bough'd beech do grow:
> Below the beeches' bough, my love,
>   Where you did never come,
> An' I don't look to meet ye now,
>   As I do look at hwome.
>
> Since now bezide my dinner-bwoard
>   Your vaice do never sound,
> I'll eat the bit I can avword,
>   A-vield upon the ground;
> Below the darksome bough, my love,
>   Where you did never dine,
> An' I don't grieve to miss ye now,
>   As I at hwome do pine.

On receipt of this Lang very handsomely lowered his point and we left the field with mutual courtesies.

Yes, and Barnes has his subtleties too. More than once you will find some queer trick of his echoed in Hardy's questioning, ironic verse and method, echoes you may catch in the following lines, which tell of a widowed man packing his poor household stuff on a waggon to transfer it to a cottage—miles away from his widowed home. Listen and recall the occasional lilt of Hardy almost at his best.

WOAK HILL

When sycamore leaves were a-spreaden
    Green-ruddy in hedges,
Bezide the red doust o' the ridges,
    A-dried at Woak Hill;

I pack'd up my goods, all a-sheenen
    Wi' long years o' handlen,
On dousty red wheels ov a waggon,
    To ride at Woak Hill.

The brown thatchen roof o' the dwellen
    I then wer a-leaven,
Had shelter'd the sleek head o' Meary,
    My bride at Woak Hill.

But now vor zome years, her light voot-vall
    'S a-lost vrom the vlooren.
Too soon vor my jay an' my childern
    She died at Woak Hill.

But still I do think that, in soul,
    She do hover about us;
To ho [care] vor her motherless childern,
    Her pride at Woak Hill.

Zoo—lest she should tell me herea'ter
    I stole off 'ithout her,
An' left her, uncall'd at house-ridden,
    To bide at Woak Hill—

I call'd her so fondly, wi' lippens
    All soundless to others,
An' took her wi' air-reachen hand
    To my zide at Woak Hill.

On the road I did look round, a-talken
    So light at my shoulder,
An' then led her in at the doorway,
    Miles wide vrom Woak Hill.

An' that's why vo'k thought, vor a season,
    My mind wer a-wanderen
Wi' sorrow, when I wer so sorely
    A-tried at Woak Hill.

But no; that my Meary mid never
    Behold herzelf, slighted,
I wanted to think that I guided
    My guide vrom Woak Hill.

XI

But I must not leave the impression that this earlier spokesman, wistful though the majority of his verses are, represents that morbidity which his greater successor—and in some ways his disciple—threw into his pictures of rustic life, largely from his own gall. Barnes's stray Eclogues of rustic chat and challenge, between ploughmen, harvesters, old 'commoners', while set in a scholar's frame, seem to me more natural, racy, lusty than anything in that form yet written in English. They have little of Pope's skill or of Landor's grace: but while Pope is Latin and Landor Hellenic, both imitative, an Eclogue of Barnes has this quiet advantage over either that it belongs to the soil as native as—forgive me, Gentlemen; I know I must follow into the trap!—as native as Burns' *The Twa Dogs*. But Barnes could be pawky too, as in *False Friends-Like*, the last poem with which I shall trouble you:

FALSE FRIENDS-LIKE

When I wer still a bwoy, an' mother's pride,
A bigger bwoy spoke up to me so kind-like,
'If you do like, I'll treat ye wi' a ride
In thease wheel-barrow here'. Zoo I wer blind-like
To what he had a-worken in his mind-like,
An' mounted vor a passenger inside;
An' comen to a puddle, perty wide,
He tipp'd me in, a-grinnen back behind-like.

Zoo when a man do come to me so thick-like,
An' sheake my hand, where woonce he pass'd me by,
An' tell me he would do me this or that,
I can't help thinken o' the big bwoy's trick-like.
An' then, vor all I can but wag my hat
An' thank en, I do veel a little shy.

XII

I have chosen to speak of this poet to-day, Gentlemen, because, having seen some revolutions in poetic fashion and in critical adjustments, I am pretty sure that recognisable poetry of whatever fashion, if it be sincere —and on that condition—endures and comes to its own, and not the less securely though it deal with the simplest commonplaces.

Take, for instance, these four lines, from *The Girt Wold House o' Mossy Stwone*—

>   The zummer air o' theos green hill
>   'V a-heav'd in buzzoms now all still,
>   An' all ther hopes an' all ther tears
>   Be unknown things ov other years.

I hope you recognise that sort of thing for poetry. Yet what could be simpler?—unless it be the artless claim that Barnes put in for that sort of thing in his Preface of 1847: thus

The author thinks his readers will find his Poems free of slang and vice, as they are written from the associations of an early youth that was passed among rural families in a secluded part of the county, upon whose sound Christian principles, kindness, and harmless cheerfulness, he can still think with complacency; and he hopes that if his little work should fall into the hands of a reader of that class in whose language it is written, it would not be likely to damp his love of God, or slacken the tone of his moral sentiment, or lower the dignity of his self-esteem.

You may smile at this. It would indeed be no excuse for bad poetry—for what I believe in the office of *The Spectator* is known as 'rectory verse'; it is no justification of good poetry, but clean beside the mark, for good poetry justifies itself.

XIII

But what may reasonably vex one is that a man who might have helped nowadays to bring our thoughts back to the poetic possibilities of rural speech in rural England, and more impressively even than John Clare (now reviving in esteem) or Thomas Ashe (who awaits revival), should deliberately have made it harder, by pedantic overlay, to recover native sincerity and preach that poetry is like the Grace of God, at once simple and Catholic and not a thing for a coterie to mince over. One can deal easily with a man who like old Thomas Nashe translates the bird-song of Spring into

   Cuckoo, jug-jug, pu-we, to-witta-woo.

But that is a different matter from entangling your

script, as Barnes does, with phonetic signs and devices. His disciple Hardy knew better. Discarding this mechanism, Hardy contrives to indicate the South-country speech by its more intimate and vital turns of phrase. So it is with such perfect conveyors of the Irish peasantry—as Miss Somerville and the late Martin Ross.

Yes, I regret that a poet so genuine as Barnes chooses to stand in his own light by his own perversity. And I doubly regret it, Gentlemen, because in these days when we hear so much about preserving rural England and the countryside, so few of our most intelligent realise that the countryside can only in the end be preserved by *living* in it, not as week-enders, but as neighbours and daily intimate friends with its people.

THE EARLIER NOVELS OF THOMAS HARDY

I

AMONG the many studies devoted to Thomas Hardy, and after the spate of journalistic *réclame* that so surprisingly burst upon us after his death and vulgarised his obsequies; I still hope, Gentlemen, that it may interest you to listen, for fifty minutes or so, to what one can recall of the impressions made by his earlier writings as they appeared—the expectations they raised, disappointed, revived—the enthusiasms he had a knack of teasing—in the breasts of many who made him a hero but found him also a grave cause of anxiety.

To be so interested you must suppose yourself at your present age, but back almost fifty years ago. You must conceive yourselves to be just as fiery and avid then for letters and the future of letters as you are to-day (surely you have imagination for that?), and moreover perhaps that you have a dream of being yourself a writer one of these days—either a very successful one or at least one whose collected works the initiate will take down from their shelf and dust more or less affectionately, saying 'this fellow could write, after all?'

The period to which you throw yourselves back, is, say, 1882–6, a four years' span of undergraduate life. Your acquaintance with Hardy began with *Far From the Madding Crowd*. You found it at school, in the Sixth Form Library; and, young as you were, it pro duced the like impression on you as James Greenwood, editor of the *Gazette*, took when—attracted by his own name in its title—he cut the opening pages of *Under the Greenwood Tree*, and felt like a man who has overed a stile upon an undiscovered country, and that yet this country was the England he had always known. You saw it now, this background of our race and its daily doings, as Greenwood saw it—with washed eyes.

Now to none of you, I hope, need I recall, to enlarge upon it, my frequent caution against handbook divisions of our literature into periods parcelled by dates or by names. Such divisions may be useful enough for examiners and lecturers, in setting out syllabuses with 'specified books' and 'books recommended'. Luckier than the courtiers of King Canute, *The Student's Guide* can command the tide 'Thus far and no farther'. But actually, of course in our literature, though a line of dry weed may mark the last impulse of a tide from which it receded, there is no searchable line in the deeps where the waters rallied and gathered. To change the simile, a man may dig a trench at the end of his garden as deep as was ever dug through England by the Conquest, or in Reformation time, or in 1642, or 1660, or (if you will) by the War of 1914–18: but the seeds carry over and germinate—as (to mention only our present author) the seed of Hardy has come across that last ditch. In fact, Gentlemen, changes in literature are always, if you search, in the air long before any book, afterwards called epoch-making, condenses them: perhaps as unconsciously as Virgil's *Pollio* Eclogue condensed the world's unconscious expectation of a Messiah.

II

Still—to compare small things with great—this man Thomas Hardy did catch and plant and acclimatise in our fiction that sensitive and 'subjective' intimacy with the country-side—its fauna, flora, contours, significant differences of scenery—which to-day is cultivated in so many literary gardens. If one quote Tennyson's

> Most can grow the flower now
> For all have got the seed

—it is with no intent at all to disparage such exquisite later cultivators as W. H. Hudson and Edward Thomas—as certainly not such genial, jovial interpreters of merry England as Messrs Belloc and Chesterton and the genius which invented or recaptured *Puck of Pook's Hill.* But the seed, as I trace back the gardening, was afloat in the early 'seventies of the last century—possibly stirred up and sent adrift unawares by Ruskin and Morris—and captured (as I see it) by Richard Jefferies and Hardy. (If you are interested in tracing the movement I recommend the pioneer books of James Owen who called himself 'A Son of the Marshes'.) I will not disparage for a moment the literary charm of these introspective observers of nature, with their reactions and fine writing: but only say that, as the grandson of an old-school naturalist who, intent on his observations, was satisfied with recording them accurately, communicating them to the notice of his fellow-scientists simply as facts illustrating the infinite and curious work of God, I prefer the way of the old school of naturalists. And who can help admiring the quiet classical close of its masterpiece, White's *Natural History of Selborne?*

When I first took the present work in hand I proposed to have added an *Annus Historico-naturalis* or the Natural History of the Twelve Months of the Year: which would have comprised many incidents and occurrences that have not fallen in my way to be mentioned in my series of letters—but as Mr Aiken of Warrington has lately published somewhat of this sort, and as the length of my correspondence has sufficiently put your patience to the test, I shall here take a respectful leave of you and natural history together, and am, with all due deference and regard, your most obliged and most humble servant.

GIL. WHITE.

Selborne,
June 25, 1787.

Or compare White's sober admiration of the Sussex Downs:

As you pass along, you command a noble view of the wild, or weald, on one hand and sea on the other. Mr Rae used to visit a family just at the foot of these hills, and was so ravished with the prospect from *Plumpton Plain*, near *Lewes*, that he mentions these scapes in his 'Wisdom of God in the Works of the Creation' with the utmost satisfaction....

Compare (I say) Mr Rae's satisfaction in his time with the personal impressions made by the Sussex Downs on Mr Hudson and Mr Thomas, or any of their many imitators, and you will at once detect the difference—difference maybe of an introspective age. For my part I enjoy this observation of natural scenery (when sincere) in relation to the writer's mood. It throws me back to certain momentary scenes of my own boyhood—to one in particular, when the sight of a green glade shelving down to a stream through Bradley Woods in Devon brought tears out of nothing but its sheer beauty, and a child's ache to run and 'tell about it'.

III

But my point here is that, in those days, while our poets had long been actively denouncing the ruin of our lovely valleys and streams, from Blake with his dark Satanic mills, to Elizabeth Barrett Browning with her *Cry of the Children*, and with Ruskin cursing the leprosy of factories, and the Pre-Raphaelites harking back to a medieval England of tapestries, ingle-nooks sackbuts, fish-ponds, and leathern bottels, these new men of the 'seventies did bring us back, in prose, to a new outlook on the rural inheritance. And I believe true what I wrote a few years ago, of some study, in prefacing a collection of English Prose, that 'It is curious to observe in contrast with our poets, who sing of green country all the time, what a disproportionate mass of our prose is *urban*, and how rarely it contrives, at the best, to get off the pavement'.

And especially is this true, if you will observe, of our novelists up to that date. They had dealt with social themes, or with romantic adventure (throwing in the ruggedness of nature, rocks and cataracts, for a background); with politics and dinner-table talk. Save for George Eliot in occasional scenes—treated with shrewdness and some feeling yet with a certain 'literary' condescension—the great ones had neglected the countryside with the human joys and woes of those who tilled it. Nor indeed was this neglect of rural life confined to the novelists. It is, up to the period of which I speak, a very curious 'missment'—to use a rural phrase—through the whole of our prose literature. Those of you who have skill in languages to follow it up, will, I hazard, find other of the prose literatures of Europe almost correspondently at fault. Even as a child in a household, whose first instinct it was of a morning, to run to the window and guess 'what the weather was going to be, where the wind sat, what the fish were likely to be doing', I seem to remember a certain dissatisfaction with so much prose literature as reached the nursery—a dissatisfaction scarcely suppressed by *The Swiss Family Robinson*, only relieved when the boy was let loose, later, upon Scott and Marryat.

The true reason may be found in this: The compelling impulse of our earlier poets was to *popularise* their themes, to *vulgarise* them (in the old and better meaning of the word, i.e. to translate them into the vulgate or English of daily converse, then rapidly ousting Norman-French or Anglo-French even among the ruling classes). Theirs was a great artistic achievement, enormously helped at its crisis by the genius of Chaucer: and as you study its artistry your admiration will increase. But the *motive* of it, apart from the adventurous joy of attempting a new thing, lay in the desire (as with Langland) to awaken Englishmen to a sense of their own worth; to interest them (as with the ballad makers) in legends of their race and its past: to translate for their enlivenment (as with Chaucer) romantic and amusing stories already current over the Continent. The England of those times being predominantly rural, an atmosphere of the country pervaded their writings: and to this the second or Elizabethan flush of our poetry of purpose occurred. Historically, for instance, we make a serious mistake if we regard Spenser first and foremost as a 'poets' poet' or a courtly one. It was part of his theory and earnest practice to revive local phrases, rustic idioms.

On the other hand our prose-writers were from the start essentially aristocratic; their audience the courtly, cultivated few. If you hunt down the list, I think you will be astonished to find, before the nineteenth century, how seldom, unless artificially or with patronage, they take the air in the green fields of England.

IV

But especially was it true of the novel when Hardy started to write—that is in or about 1870, the year of Dickens' death. Now the blaze of Dickens' genius not only shrivelled and ate up (for the general good) a growth of low-class Cockney fiction—Samuel Warren's *Ten Thousand a Year*, Albert Smith's *Christopher Tadpole* and that sort of thing: it killed for years the very seed of it. Called in his life 'the inimitable', he left no school, though he influenced many here and over Europe; and I think you will agree that his individuality could have been bequeathed to no school. Thackeray, on the other hand, came of a long tradition which he left improved. In 1870, for example, George Eliot was writing *Middlemarch*, George Meredith *The Adventures of Harry Richmond*, and Trollope filling an industrious interval between the Barchester novels and *The Eustace Diamonds*. So, even after the success of *Far From the Madding Crowd* backed the possibly less popular but recognised artistic success of *Under the*

Greenwood Tree, we find Hardy all a-twitter over the supposed and distasteful obligation to take—as one may put it—a course in society manners to qualify as a novelist. To confirm this, let me quote one passage from *The Early Life of Thomas Hardy* so carefully compiled, so delicately yet penetratingly written, by his second wife.

He was now committed by circumstances to novel-writing as a regular trade, as much as he had previously been to architecture; and that hence he would, he deemed, have to look for material in *manners*—in ordinary social and fashionable life as other novelists did. Yet he took no interest in manners, but in the substance of life only. So far what he had written had not been novels at all—as usually understood—that is pictures of modern customs and observances—and might not long sustain the interest of the circulating library subscriber who cared mainly for those things. On the other hand, to go about to dinners and clubs and crowds as a business was not to his mind. Yet that was necessary meat and drink to the popular author. Not that he was unsociable, but events and long habit had accustomed him to solitary living.... He mentioned this doubt of himself one day to Miss Thackeray, who confirmed his gloomy misgivings by saying with surprise: 'Certainly: a novelist must necessarily like society!'

V

Well, Gentlemen, you surely see how stupid all that is: how excusable, if commercial, in a young man throwing the dice with fortune: how unworthy, however coupled with a mind already nursing the germ of *The Dynasts*. One of these days science, exploring history, may render some account to us of what the world's sum of poetry— its most priceless possession—has lost through its poets' eternal lack of pence—though I hope it never can, our world being sad enough, just now, without that information. But you probably divine how this 'inferiority complex' debilitated many of Hardy's earlier novels. Let me record how his early worshippers felt it. 'Here is a man', we felt, 'capable of lifting the English novel out of a social rut. Passage after passage proves that he can write pure, melodious prose: but, more than this, passage after passage suggests that here is a universal man, with a sense of the stars in their immensity, with a sense of his own and his neighbour's pulse and its harmony with them'. 'He could not go on for ever writing about shepherds?' No, for his mind was stretching out all the while to grasp and interpret Napoleon as a puppet of fate: instead of which he must bother himself about the troubles of a woman in society whose father, as butler, is sedately pouring champagne across her shoulder. Well, that is a situation which Meredith could have managed—as no reader of *Evan Harrington* will doubt. Meredith would have made the guests talk fantastically, as no company ever did talk or, it is to be hoped, ever could. His are conversational exercises in fancy dress: but the point is, the interlocutors *do* wear their fancy dress as if it fitted them and they had no awkwardness in it. Nor is it insincere, inasmuch as it comes straight from the author's disposition and demands your willing suspension of disbelief, almost a *credo quia impossibile* such as you carry away from the Mad Hatter's Tea-party. The converse of Hardy's society people does not fit in this way; and —which is worse—you feel that they do not fit Hardy; that he has bought a suit of clothes to come to the party.

To be sure, when you think of it, Agamemnon never talked in hexameters, nor Virgil in *terza rima*, nor Coriolanus in blank verse, nor Phaedra in Alexandrines: but you are made to forget they did not. The conversation of 'ladies' and 'gentlemen' in these earlier novels (to which I confine myself) too often goes on stilts with occasional and distressing tumbles, as when, in *Two on a Tower*—a story that just misses the idyllic best by stilted talk between amorous lips—Louis Glanville lets us and his sister Lady Constantine down together by adjuring her not to be such a 'flat' as to refuse her hand in marriage when the Bishop has 'popped'.

VI

I am anticipating, however. Let us revert to the position for which I invited your curiosity—that of a young admirer who, arrested by *Far From the Madding Crowd* and fascinated as by something new and strange, sought back for all its author had previously written, and, possessed of this, became, as further books appeared, his constant reader; often delighted, almost as often perplexed, sometimes faint, but always pursuing. Take it, if you will, as cautionary: a study in unwisdom before the event. You all know now, as we did not know then, that Hardy, a struggling architect and writer of unsaleable poetry—an accepted and devoted lover, but with small prospect of earning enough by his profession to support a wife—turned to fiction as a sort of 'desperate remedy' with little sense of it as yet as a fine and difficult art, and—one may assert—with small aptitude for it as he understood it.

We know the story of his first attempt—of the novel which did not survive. He entitled it *The Poor Man and the Lady—by the Poor Man*, and he sent the MS. first to Mr Alexander Macmillan who consulted with John Morley upon it. They agreed that the performance was 'very curious and original', that the writer had stuff and purpose in him, that certain of the scenes were wildly extravagant 'so that they read like some clever lad's dream' and that the book in short was unsaleable. Hardy then visited Messrs Chapman and Hall with the MS. under his arm. That firm turned it over to their 'reader', George Meredith; who by-and-by gave the author an interview and advised him in substance that the book was raw and violent—in fact a sweeping dramatic satire of the squirearchy and nobility, London society, the vulgarity of the middle class, modern Christianity, church restoration, and political and domestic morals in general. It sounds fairly comprehensive.

No one knows what afterwards became of the MS. But I think we may gather—if only from the title itself—that Hardy was already possessed with a self-conscious indignation which distressed and haunted him almost throughout his life, breaks out again and again in his novels, takes charge of some, and finally explodes in *Jude the Obscure*; at a time of life when he might have known by unprejudiced observation that if

> Slow rises worth by poverty depressed,

the last place to search for illustration of this mournful truth would be one or other of our ancient Universities, which, if any seminaries on earth do in my observation —now continued over many years—present at least the best-known realisation of a democracy, and reduce (whether by encouragement or by kicks) a young man to the level of his worth.

But we deal here with Hardy's earlier novels. The figure of a young man of genius, conscious of his power but awkward and diffident in company—in dreams a king, but, waking, no such matter—is familiar enough in literary annals; as is the tragedy of some who have mistaken the patronage of 'noble dames' for a warmer personal interest. From this misfortune we may allow that Hardy was saved by an early and passionate attachment. That yet he was born and bred liable to it—that the shadow of it dogged him—may, I think, be read into tale after tale of his, that contrive tragedy on the complication of a luxurious woman's fancy for a man below her in rank or wealth. I choose to-day, not for convenience' sake but for a reason we shall consider, to draw a dividing line at *Two on a Tower*. But this *imbroglio* persists beyond that book and breeds the disease of *The Woodlanders* (to my thinking his loveliest if not his strongest book), as of many a later short story.

VII

Balanced with this you have his uncanny, suspicious sense of the *other woman's* motives in loving. It has been said that 'every woman sees a home through her engagement ring'. Possibly. *Mutatis mutandis*, the same may be said of birds. But that women in love bring quite such a calculating eye to it as (for one example of many) does Fancy Day in *Under the Greenwood*

Tree; that they have quite such second thoughts as she shares with the heroines of *A Pair of Blue Eyes* and *A Laodicean*, with Ethelberta or even with *Eustacia Vye* in the intervals of her passion, few men before Hardy had been apt to guess, no women willing to allow. Certainly I can think of no writer, before or since, who rings the changes as Hardy does on the *arrière-pensées* of the well-beloved: and there my nescience must leave you with the fact that while he wrote anonymously he was generally accused, by female readers, of being a woman or, alternatively, of knowing too much.

So let us leave it at that—with one addition which I should be loth to make, had he not patently and admittedly taken the world into confidence of his own courtship—time, place, person, circumstance—in the story *A Pair of Blue Eyes*, and also in many a dated lyric. It will probably never be disclosed by the hand which has so delicately written the story of his early life —and yet there seems no harm in telling an innocent thing of which all who had privilege of converse with him in his last years were reverently aware—that his widowhood had constructed a pure fairy-tale of that youthful time, bathed in romantic colour: that the mere presence of one familiar with those scenes, the houses he had visited on his honeymoon, the families and the tale of their descendants; where this love-lane led or that farm had decayed—with such an auditor to assure or prompt a memory he would sit happy, retracing, always reclothing, dressing up, the dream. Actually his first wife, to those who met her, was a woman of remarkably strong character, difficult, straightly loyal, for years distrustful that novel-writing was not quite the occupation to which this queer wonderful husband of hers should demean himself; she herself being connected with the clergy—niece, indeed, to an Archdeacon.

VIII

Now set this against Hardy's authenticated taking to fiction at first as a means of livelihood. Set against it or beside it the fact (now known to all) that secretly from the first he was a poet, though an unaccepted and a baffled one: and we face the paradox which, explicable now, in those early years perplexed and, time and again, disheartened the devotee. *Desperate Remedies* to start with (though few of us had read it); then *Under the Greenwood Tree* (so nearly perfect); then *A Pair of Blue Eyes* with its emotional uncertainty and stage tricks in dialogue and structure; then *Far From the Madding Crowd* and the feeling that genius had all but found itself; then a disconcerting let-down with *The Hand of Ethelberta*; a tremendous recovery with *The Return of the Native* and the triumph apparently assured; a happy pause on the level with *The Trumpet Major*; and then—the plumb pitfall of *A Laodicean*. We knew not then of this mysterious writer (how could we?) as we learned at long later, that the major part of *A Laodicean* had been dictated from a sick bed in intervals of pain and haemorrhage, heroically, to fulfil a signed contract: but to anyone then unknowing—

> The moving finger writes: and, having writ,
> Moves on...

with what a zig-zag left on the chart!

Let us go back and observe how Meredith has sent Hardy away, advising him to attempt something with a more 'complicated' plot. You, who know your *Poetics*, will guess (as one who has heard Meredith's talk may pretty well assure you) that he airily used that Aristotelian term 'complicated plot' assuming that Hardy understood. Hardy goes away supposing that by 'complicated' is meant 'sensational *plus* intricate', after the fashion of Wilkie Collins, Mrs Henry Wood, Miss Braddon,..., authors just then in vogue—yes, and in their way, let me assure you, as artists by no means to be despised. If any young aspirant in fiction nowadays care to study the *anatomy* of the business, let him spend study on Wilkie Collins' *Moonstone*; or let him take a forgotten tale by Miss Braddon, *Henry Dunbar*, strip it to the bone, and he will discover an anatomy quite Sophoclean in the story of a daughter sworn to hunt down her father's murderer, tracking him to bay to discover that the murderer is her father himself! All the material of Sophoclean irony is there under the muslin flounces.

Hardy then, mistaking Meredith, attempts a 'sensational' novel, which complicates it, with the result of *Desperate Remedies*. It is obvious that, whatever the talent of this young man as an architect, he started with little for constructing a plot. This and succeeding novels are full (to keep the architectural simile) of stays, struts and buttresses, hasty props, balances to keep the building solid, even plasterings to cover mistakes—or, in plain words, of coincidences, intercepted letters, interferences by convulsion of nature, audible soliloquies, stage asides and eaves-droppings. The eaves-droppings, for example—overhearings of secret conversations for furtherance of the plot—in these earlier novels have only to be counted to suggest some strange youthful ailment after being separately dismissed as incredible. Twice at least the whole intrigue of *A Laodicean* violates probability, but, as we know, *A Laodicean* was dictated in sickness, so let us take an earlier specimen. A brother and sister are exchanging confidences: on the other side of a hedge a malignant woman is tracking them—

> Their conversation [says the story], of which every word was clear and distinct, in the still air of the dawn, to the distance of a quarter of a mile, reached her ears.

[Lecturers, please copy!]
    Again—

> 'Do you believe in such odd coincidences?' said Cytherea.
> 'How do you mean? [sic] They occur sometimes.'

They occur, indeed, so often that, opening a chapter headed precisely, 'From Ten to Half-past Eleven p.m.', we read without any amazement—

> 'A strange concurrence of phenomena now confronts us.'

IX

Yes, but wait a moment! Meredith, while rejecting *The Poor Man and the Lady*, had noted in it a certain knack with circumstantial detail, used to convey a sense of events actually happening, in the way of Defoe, curiously reminiscent of Defoe. Therefore, after wasting

THOMAS HARDY 213

this moment, do not waste another over that silly sentence and confession of inept design—'A strange concurrence of phenomena now confronts us'—but read straight on into the description of the fire at the Tranter's, how it grew step by step from smouldering to a fierce blaze (four pages of it), and I am mistaken if, in the long range of English fiction between Defoe and Hardy, you will find anything *just like that*. Then compare this fire, if you will, with that in *Far From the Madding Crowd*, and note how man's strength and will is brought into the epic. Consider next (I but offer this as one clue for your curiosity) the famous lay-out of Egdon Heath in *The Return of the Native*. Read it by the light of an entry in his note-book under date September 28, 1877—

An object or mark raised or made by man on a scene is worth ten times any such formed by unconscious Nature. Hence clouds, mists and mountains are unimportant beside the wear on a threshold, or the print of a hand.

Set this beside an earlier declaration—

The poetry of a scene varies with the minds of the perceivers. Indeed it does not lie in the scene at all.

and you have some bearing (I think) on the development of the epic passages in the Novel—as played with by Fielding, occasionally gripped by the Brontës, elaborated by Reade, by the Kingsleys—to name none later—but born in Scott and Dickens, well grasped by Hardy and, when you come to size them, letting loose upon conventional technique force that gives *magnitude*: as it did with Cervantes and later with Tolstoy.

X

Yet as I read Hardy's earlier novels over again the secret of his later ones seems in some measure to explain itself. Suddenly, by a page or two in *Two on a Tower*—a page or two at which story I have chosen to draw a line between his earlier and later work; a shadowy line, I must admit: as shadowy perhaps as any line traceable between literary 'periods'. To me some pages of *Two on a Tower* provide almost a touch-stone of that kind of genius (Shakespeare's for a palmary instance) which explodes in any number of different directions before disclosing the central fire. Anyhow, the crucial pages for me in Hardy's development are those in which he opens, through the lips of an immature astronomer, the illimitable depths and despair of the heavens. Listen to a few words only of his—

> And to add a new weirdness to what the sky possesses in its size and formlessness there is involved the quality of decay. For all the wonder of these everlasting spheres, eternal stars and what not, they are not eternal: they burn out like candles. You see that dying one in the body of the Greater Bear. Two centuries ago it was as bright as the others. The senses may become terrified by plunging among them and they are, but there is a pitifulness even in their glory. Imagine them all extinguished, and a mind feeling its way through a heaven of total darkness, occasionally striking against the black invisible cinders of those stars. If you are cheerful, and wish to remain so, leave the study of astronomy alone. Of all sciences, it alone deserves the character of the terrible.

Now you know, Gentlemen, that the old educational course of the Middle Ages, as we call them, divided itself into the elementary, or *Trivium*, consisting of Grammar, Rhetoric and Dialectic; and the more advanced *Quadrivium*, embracing Music, Arithmetic, Geometry and Astronomy.

Well, now not speaking as an Educational Reformer (Heaven forbid!) I have sometimes wondered if some acquaintance with astronomy ought not to be a compulsory part of any gentleman's education. It would, I think, most profitably correct any sense of his own importance in the scheme of things and, by consequence, soften his manners through such a phase as he inherits on this little planet. The test is, knowing yourself a man, to face these immensities and not to be frightened: to recognise that there are still friends about you, counsellors—Plato for instance—and that, if you stand steady, the swing of the Universe goes round 'on time', the angels are in the sentry boxes, and your own little pulse without any of your own stupid interference ticking away in tune.

This regulating purpose is just what Hardy cannot recognise. He has looked into those inter-stellar depths, realised them, with a shudder, and so far as he has done this his novels are 'universal', but only so far: for in the dazzle he sees but anomalies, odds and ends, misfits, blind alleys, cast off pluckings (damnably painful to the victims) from the web that, to no evident pattern or purpose, a drowsy immanent Will goes on shuttling, weaving.

XI

But just here comes in the paradox and the smiling irony of the Gods upon their rebel and declared ironeïst. This man, taking up the trade of fiction with no great zest, certainly under the urgency of no clear call, learns to achieve success; and promptly, to the dismay of his publishers, turns away from it to attempt new things—and this not once, but sundry times. He deems himself to be choosing, while actually he is being driven by the unsatisfied poet implanted within him. Accusing what he calls the Immanent Will, or President of the Immortals, of weaving life without a purpose, or even of fashioning it as in mockery as *hocus-pocus*, he lays down his pen on that final taunt in *Tess*, and takes up another, still unaware that he himself has been working to pattern all the while, and by working the pattern out has won the poet's emancipation, leisure, and with leisure power, to write *The Dynasts*. All the while of course the poet within him was struggling: and it seems to me characteristic that, although he sometimes dated his lyrics, sometimes jotted down the place of composition so that the date can be sought out by us, his own memory concerning their time and order as often as not found itself at fault, so that, even with aid of these insufficient *data*, the casual reader might easily mistake him for a pessimist born and to the end untaught by enterprise, enquiry or event. Let me give just one personal anecdote to illustrate this. The last letter he wrote me, not long before his death, put the staggering question 'Why had I [in a certain anthology called the *Oxford Book of English Verse*] preferred certain poems—call them *A*, *B* and *C*—to *X*, *Y* and *Z* which, on reflection, I must surely acknowledge to be better'. To which, of course, the simple answer had to be that in 1900—the date of my selection—these better lyrics did not happen to have been given to the world, and —though you put a murrain on his business—the poor anthologist cannot ply his trade upon things non-existent, or, at any rate, non-apparent. And I conclude upon this little story as on a parable.

TRIBUTE TO IRELAND

IT is sad to look on the title-page of *Irish Memories*, and sorrowful to realise that it is the last on which we shall see the joyous names of E. Œ. Somerville and Martin Ross coupled together. It was bound to be sorrowful whenever it happened; but in these days we have too little of the salt of life and a great need of it. Death has divided these two ladies, whom no critic poring over their books could separate. We say 'poring', because the stories have this of 'classical' quality—that while thousands of ordinary folk read them for sheer delight and the fun of it, and the hunting man and the Irishman recur to them affectionately, recognising their knowledge of the sport and the people 'from the heart out', a man whose business is with the art of story-telling may study them with ever-renewed wonder, marking page after page on which not a sentence can be spared nor a half-dozen words rearranged without spoiling 'the sweet wild twist of the song'.

Miss Somerville has not let us into the secret, probably because she could not—it is incommunicable. Nor does she do more than tease our wonder, which is everybody's, at the unity of style she and Martin Ross achieved. On this point she reduces curiosity to a unity of folly. We are one with the babbling lady who asked—

'Are *you* the Miss Somerville who writes the books with Miss Martin? To think that I should have been talking to you all this time! And is it you that do the story and Miss Martin the words?' (&c., &c., for some time.) 'And which of you holds the pen?... And do you put in everyone you meet? No? Only sometimes? And sometimes people whom you *never* meet. Well! I declare it looks like direct inspiration!'

and equally we are one with Andrew Lang:

To me then Andrew L. with a sort of off-hand fling, 'I suppose you're the one who does the writing?' I explained with some care that it was not so. He said he didn't know how any two people could equally evolve characters, &c.; that he had tried, and it was always the other who did it all. I said I didn't know how we managed, but anyhow that I knew little of bookmaking as a science. He said I must know a good deal.

All the secret would seem to lie in a sympathy of close friendship, to which many pages of this book bear witness, shining and tender, almost too holy to quote—and of blood relationship. The mothers of Miss Somerville and Martin Ross (Violet Florence Martin) were first cousins, grand-daughters of Chief Justice Bushe, the 'incorruptible', who had opposed the Act of Union with noble eloquence, and left the Irish House of Commons ringing to the words, 'I ask you, gentlemen, will you give up your country?'

In Ireland it is not so much Love that hath us in its net as Relationship. Pedigree takes precedence even of politics, and in all affairs that matter it governs unquestioned.... There was once a high magnate of a self-satisfied provincial town (its identity is negligible). An exhibition was presently to be held there, and it chanced that a visit from Royalty occurred shortly before.... It also chanced that a possible visit to Ireland of a still greater personage impended.... The lesser Royalty partook of lunch with the magnate, and the latter broached the question of a State opening of the exhibition by the august visitor to be. 'When ye go back to London now', he beguiled, 'coax the Brother!'

We shall recur to our two ladies' kinship, having anticipated the story here because it may help to explain—as, for certain, nothing else explains—the close working of two minds.

On other points Miss Somerville is more explicit. Some readers with 'Philippa's Fox-hunt' in their minds, or the great *peripeteia* of 'Lisheen Races'—when Driscoll, the supposed defunct, comes roaring in search of Slipper ('Show me Slipper!... Show me that dirty little undherlooper till I have his blood! Hadn't I the race won only for he souring the mare on me! What's that you say? I tell ye he did! He left seven slaps on her with the handle of a hay-rake'); some readers again, recalling the pack of hounds delivered to Mr Freddy Alexander at Craffroe railway station ('I have them gethered in the Ladies' Waiting-room, Sir, the way ye'll have no trouble. 'Twould be as good for yer to lave the muzzles on them till ye'll be through the town'), or the famous run with Mr Robert Trinder's 'Rioters' (starting from the mansion which 'had looked decidedly better in large red letters at the top of old Robert's notepaper than it did at the top of his lawn—a house, as his aunt put it, "rotten with dogs"'—and sweeping through incredible adventures to the release of a puppy from a tin can), will blush uneasily, contritely may be, when they reach the page on which Miss Somerville protests against the epithet 'rollicking'. Lever was 'rollicking'; to rollick was of his period and that of Surtees. As for Surtees, 'no one who has ever ridden a hunt or loved a hound but must admit that he has his unsurpassable moments'—'The cat and custard-pot day', for example:

TRIBUTE TO IRELAND

But I think it is undeniable that the hunting people of Handley Cross, like Lever's dragoons, were always at full gallop. With Surtees, as with Lever, every one is 'all out', there is nothing in hand—save perhaps a pair of duelling pistols or a tandem whip.... That intolerable adjective 'rollicking' is consecrated to Lever; if certain of the rank and file of the reviewers of our later books could have realized with what abhorrence we found it applied to ourselves, and could have known how rigorously we endeavoured to purge our work of anything that might justify it, they might, out of the kindness that they have always shown us, have been more sparing of it.

Well, let us say 'frolicking'. But Martin Ross, as Captain Stephen Gwynn puts it in a letter, was never of those who can be content to regard Ireland as a pleasant place for sport, full of easy, laughable people; or she would never have understood Ireland with that intensity which can be felt even in her humour. If her letters show that she was often angry with her countrymen, they show too that it was because she could not be indifferent to the honour of Ireland.

On another point of their craft, the literary rendering of 'dialect', Miss Somerville says an eminently wise word:

Phonetic spelling in matters of dialect is a delusive thing, to be used with the utmost restraint. It is superfluous for those who know, boring for those who do not. Of what avail is spelling when confronted with the problem of indicating the pronunciation of, for example, 'Papa'; the slurring and softening of the consonant, the flattening of the vowel sound—how can these be even indicated? And, spelling or no, can any tongue save an Irish one pronounce the words 'being' and 'ideal' as though they owned but one syllable? Long ago Martin and I debated the point, and the conclusion that we then arrived at was that the root of the matter in questions of dialect was in the idiomatic phrase and the mental attitude. The doctrine of 'Alice's' friend, the Duchess, still seems to me the only safe guide. 'Take care of the sense, and the sounds will take care of themselves.'

We have laid stress on these shy revelations of their craft because the authors of *The Irish R.M.* were in truth artists to their finger-tips, with an art so cunning to conceal itself that not one reader in ten, perhaps, guesses with what skill he is being ridden, the hands lie so delicately on the rein. And this book of memories is not less skilful than its forerunners, for all its seeming desultoriness. It opens with some chapters on the history of the Martins of Ross, a beautiful old Irish estate by a lake-side in the west of Galway. 'Herself', as Miss Somerville would say, left this account among her papers, having designed it for a memoir of her eldest brother Robert, who died in 1905. It abounds in vivid pictures of the famine years, of the old squirearchy of Ireland, tender and impossible, in the days of its sunsetting, in gay portraits of innumerable relatives, all men and women of character and the most of them extravagantly odd. When Miss Somerville arrives from *her* ancestral home above the rocks of Carbery, Co. Cork, and takes up the wondrous tale, the gallery becomes fairly bewildering. The families ran as a rule to prodigious length, Martin Ross herself being an eleventh daughter: but, as a cousin of hers was consoled, a mother of but two children—boy and girl, 'Afther all, if ye had a hundhred of them ye couldn't have a greater variety'. We range from Thomas Somerville, first of his family to settle in Munster, who reposes under a slab proclaiming him 'A worthy Magistrate and a Safe and Affable Companion', to Chief Justice Bushe; to Robert Ross, Martin's grandfather, who in frock coat and top hat mounted a refractory horse in a dealer's yard in Dublin 'and took him round St Stephen's Green at a gallop through the traffic, laying into him with his umbrella'; to Maria Edgeworth; to a female cousin of Martin's who objected to Shakespeare ('Shakespeare was a coarse man, my dear, but you may read him to me if you like. I can go into a reverie'); to Miss Somerville's cousin, Mrs Pierrepont Mundy, 'a very delightful letter-writer and story-teller, who has taken with her to the next world a collection of anecdotes that may possibly cause her relatives there to share the regret of her friends here that she did not leave them behind her'; to Cousin Nannie, who had a strong sense of the ridiculous and a singularly small and well-shaped foot on which the shoe-strings had a habit of coming untied.

She returned to her family one day and related with joy how, as she passed a cabstand, her shoelace had become unfastened, and how she had then asked a cabman to tie it for her. She thanked him with her usual and special skill in such matters, and, as she slowly moved away, she was pleased to hear her cabman remark to a fellow:
'That's a dam pleasant owld heifer!'
And the response of the fellow:
'Ah, Shakespeare says ye'll always know a rale lady when ye see her'.

Nor, if a gentle criticism may be allowed, does the chronicle lack a certain very feminine perversity. The original Martins were staunch Roman Catholics. At one point they changed their religion, which was a stiff thing to do and involved a certain change of politics. Martin Ross records this equably, and thenceforth as equably shifts her own point of view. Again, of 'the Chief'—Bushe—who fought the Union to the last ditch, our authoresses, rightly and properly, speak in terms but a little 'this side idolatry'. For the men, however, who, eighty years later, started to re-win the lost battle they can find no terms too severe. But relationship in Ireland is, as they tell us, everything. Gracious indeed and lovable must have been the old feudal rule at Ross and on many another estate. Who can blame them for commemorating it fondly?

That the larger landowners were as a class honourable, reasonably fair-minded, and generous as is not on the whole disputed, is a credit to their native kindliness and good breeding. They had neither public opinion nor legal restraint to interfere with them. Each estate was a kingdom, and, in the impossibility of locomotion, each neighbouring potentate acquired a relative importance quite out of proportion to his merits; for to love your neighbour—or, at all events, to marry her—was almost inevitable when matches were a matter of mileage and marriages might be said to have been made by the map.

Feuds, too, in such a society would by inbreeding become inveterate. 'Fights were made, like the wall-papers, the carpets, the furniture, to last'. But on the whole the picture rendered radiates a noble charity, a careless splendour with a sense of high responsibility—best of all, of *understanding*. We suppose that no class in this world ever justified itself more humanly than did these resident Irish landowners during the famine years. But what of the absentees?

Though the descendants of Chief Justice Bushe—Bushes, Plunkets, Coghills, Foxes, Franks, Harrises—might say, 'Dublin is my washpot, over Merrion-square will I cast my shoe'; though this book has much to tell of Bohemian days in Paris, in the Latin Quarter; though it narrates happy excursions to Oxford, to St Andrews—it is to their own poor folk in Cork and Galway that Miss Somerville and Miss Martin owed the understanding which we recognise as genius. No such understanding could have come to them (to quote a cousin's phrase) by a *ventre à terre* at Dublin—even at Dublin. Theirs is 'racy', and, so far as a stranger may judge, impeccable.

It is generally known, of course, that Miss Somerville has been a redoubtable M.F.H. Some know that Martin Ross, though incurably short-sighted, carried the heart of a lion against fences she but dimly discerned. Few know that she lay an invalid for years after a hunting accident, and that in the most famous of the books, *The Irish R.M.*, she collaborated on a bed of nervous torture. These *Memories* contain a chapter on Dogs and another on Horses and Hounds, and in the latter will be found vignettes as entrancing as any of the old tales. Miss Somerville took over the Mastership of the West Carbery pack in 1903 from her brother, of whom it was said that among the country people 'he was the King of the world for them! If he rode his horses into their beds they'd ask no better'. A difficult country, one may conjecture, trusting to the account of an American lady for whom the West Carbery put up a 'ringing' fox, who rather over-did his anxiety to show the visitor a typical West Carbery line and 'declined to demonstrate the fact that we possessed any grass country':

Our visitor held the hunt, such as it was, with the best, and spoke with marked enthusiasm of the agility of our horses. Later I heard her discussing the events of the day.

'We jumped one place', said my visitor, 'and I said to myself, "Well, I suppose that never on God's earth shall I see a thing like that again!" And after that', she went on, 'we jumped it five times'.

Miss Somerville is eloquent upon her hunters—Lottery, Kitty, Tarbrush, a black but comely lady, 'a jumper in earnest, who would face up and beyond anything she could see', and would, if perturbed in temper, go very near to 'kicking the stars out of the sky'; and, above all, Bridget, daughter of a thoroughbred sire and a Bantry mountain pony.

'She has a plain head', said a rival horse-coper, who had been so unfortunate as not to have seen her before I did, 'but that suits the rest of her.'

The best pages of the book are those upon which criticism must not intrude, for they enshrine the memory of Martin Ross—slight, fair to see, refined of intellect and body, true Irish, indomitably brave, indomitably gay. Let us conclude with the benediction bestowed upon her by a beggar-woman in Skibbereen: 'Sure, ye're always laughing! That ye may laugh in the sight of the Glory of Heaven'.

INDEX

Abercrombie, Lascelles, 80
Addison, Joseph, 79
Admetus, 51
Adventures of Harry Richmond, The, 203
Aeschylus, 13, 17, 112
Alcaeus, 9
Alcestis, 97
Alcibiades, 91
Alexander, 9
Alford, Henry, 161
All's Well that Ends Well, 146, 152
Andersen, Hans, 154
Apocrypha, 47
Arden, Mary, 159
Aretino, Peter of, 78
Aristotle, 21, 25, 33, 37, 73, 77, 86, 87, 90, 91, 92, 93, 95, 97, 104, 133, 134, 144
Arnold, Matthew, 14, 15, 34, 38, 74, 79, 92, 177
Ashe, Thomas, 195
As You Like It, 137
Athanasius, 49
Aurelius, Marcus, 32, 42
Austen, Jane, 178

Bacchae, 7
Bacon, Francis, 4, 35, 63, 70
Bagehot, Walter, 3
Balzac, 178
Barnes, William, 174 *et seq.*
Bates, H. E., 59
Beethoven, 79
Belloc, Hilaire, 199
Berkeley, George, 63
Bible, The, 19, 20, 86, 98
Biographia Literaria, 67, 68, 70, 71, 72
Blake, William, 63, 79, 125, 201
Blakesley, J. W., 161
Bloomfield, Robert, 183
Bradby, G. F., 76
Braddon, Miss, 211
Bradley, A. C., 155
Bridges, Robert, 36, 73

Brontës, the, 213
Brooke, Rupert, 161
Brotherton, Mrs, 166
Browning, Elizabeth Barrett, 201
Browning, Robert, 113, 181
Buller, Charles, 162
Burke, Edmund, 70
Burns, Robert, 14, 74, 168, 184, 185, 186, 190, 193
Bushe, Chief Justice, 219, 223, 224, 225
Butler, Samuel, 63
Byron, Lord, 28, 63, 165, 166, 167

Calderon, 167
Calidara, 167
Calvin, John, 27
Carducci, 13
Carlyle, Thomas, 30, 31
Carr, Wildon, 78, 79
Castelvetro, 88, 89
Cervantes, 213
Chambers, Sir Edmund, 159
Chaucer, 63, 74, 78, 189, 202
Chesterton, G. K., 199
Cicero, 75
Clare, John, 183, 195
Clough, Arthur Hugh, 31
Cobbett, William, 190
Coleridge, Mary, 142
Coleridge, Samuel Taylor, 37, 63, 67, 68, 69, 70, 71, 72, 74, 79, 166, 167, 168, 171
Collins, Wilkie, 185, 211
Columbus, Christopher, 62
Condell, Henry, 132
Cowley, Abraham, 181
Croce, Benedetto, 76, 77, 80, 89
Cromwell, Oliver, 31
Cymbeline, 147

Dallas, Eneas Sweetland, 4, 6, 30, 32, 89
Dante, 13, 50, 71, 74, 79, 121
Darwin, Erasmus, 63, 115
Defoe, Daniel, 212, 213

228   INDEX

Dekker, Thomas, 124
Dickens, Charles, 63, 178, 203, 213
Diderot, Denis, 32
Diodorus, 9
Disraeli, Benjamin, 32, 178
Donne, John, 27
Doughty, C. M., 36
Dryden, John, 13, 63, 73, 79, 88

Eldon, Lord, 43
Eliot, George, 36, 201, 203
Eliot, T. S., 44 et seq., 74–5, 79, 121
Emerson, Ralph Waldo, 32
Euripides, 12, 18
Everyman, 102, 146

Fielding, Henry, 63, 116, 178, 213
Firdausi, 167
FitzGerald, Edward, 169, 170
Frederick of Prussia, 31
Froude, Hurrell, 53

Gibbon, Edward, 12
Gladstone, William Ewart, 162
Goethe, 13
Goldsmith, Oliver, 2
Gray, Thomas, 185
Greene, Robert, 1
Greenwood, James, 198
Gwynn, Stephen, 221

Hallam, Arthur Henry, 161, 162, 163, 167
Hamlet, 113, 148, 154, 155
Hardy, Thomas, 36, 37, 38, 177, 178, 185, 191, 196, 197 et seq.
Harrington, James, 39
Hartley, David, 67, 71, 72
Harvey, William, 41
Hazlitt, William, 14, 74
Heath, Douglas, 162
Hegel, 79
Heminge, John, 132
Henry the Sixth, 149
Herbert, George, 27, 48
Herodotus, 9
Herrick, Robert, 15, 179
Heywood, Thomas, 2
Hobbes, Thomas, 27
Homer, 2, 74, 108, 112, 117, 118, 167
Hood, Thomas, 81 et seq.

Hooker, Richard, 70
Horace, 8, 15, 16, 39, 87
Houghton, Lord, 162
Hudson, William Henry, 199, 200
Hugo, Victor, 13
Hunt, Leigh, 166

Iliad, The, 17, 117
Inge, W. R., 141

Jackson, Henry, 66
James, Henry, 61
Jefferies, Richard, 199
Johnson, Samuel, 3, 13, 63, 73, 79, 80, 88, 130, 181
Jones, Ernest, 155
Jonson, Ben, 13, 14, 79, 132
Julius Caesar, 147

Kant, 79
Keats, John, 5, 14, 15, 81, 84, 164, 166
Kemble, John Mitchell, 162
Ker, W. P., 95
King Lear, 118, 148, 154, 156, 158
Kingsleys, the, 213
Knight, Charles, 122

Lamb, Charles, 14, 74, 79, 150
Landor, Walter Savage, 15, 18, 23, 37, 63, 120, 121, 166, 193
Lang, Andrew, 185, 191, 219
Langland, William, 63, 202
Lecky, W. E. H., 141, 142
Lee, Sir Sidney, 159
Lessing, 89, 105, 114, 115, 117, 119
Lewes, George Henry, 89
Locke, John, 63
Longfellow, Henry Wadsworth, 117
Longinus, 98
Love's Labour's Lost, 125, 146
Lucretius, 13
Lushingtons, the, 162
Lytton, Bulwer, 165

Macaulay, Thomas Babington, 30
Macbeth, 124
Maccabees, Second Book of, 47
McLennan, John Ferguson, 137
Macmillan, Alexander, 207
Maine, Sir Henry, 137, 138

INDEX

Marlowe, Christopher, 1
Marryat, Frederick, 202
Marvell, Andrew, 124, 145
Maurois, André, 31
Merchant of Venice, The, 73, 151
Meredith, George, 36, 133, 203, 205, 207
Merivale, Charles, 161
Michelangelo, 13, 79
Midsummer Night's Dream, 146
Milnes, Richard Monckton, 162
Milton, John, 13, 26, 27, 63, 64, 65, 79, 89, 99, 100
Moore, Thomas, 165
Morgan, Lewis Henry, 137
Morley, John, 32, 207
Morris, William, 199

Napoleon III, 176
Nashe, Thomas, 195
Nelson, Lord, 8, 74
Newbolt, Sir Henry, 96
Newman, John Henry, 31, 53, 54, 55, 56, 63, 89
Newton, Sir Isaac, 63

Odyssey, The, 17, 118
Oedipus, 91, 158
Owen, James, 199

Paley, Frederick, 95
Palgrave, Francis, 179
Palmer, William, 52, 53, 55, 56
Pascal, 65
Patmore, Coventry, 79
Patria Potestas, 137, 144
Paul, St, 42, 139
Peacock, Thomas Love, 178
Peele, George, 1
Phillipps, Halliwell, 159
Pilgrim Fathers, 48
Pindar, 13, 17, 18
Plato, 2, 4, 18, 19, 40, 63
Plutarch, 32, 33, 114
Poe, Edgar Allen, 89
Poetics, Aristotle's, 25, 40, 86 *et seq.*, 133, 144, 211
Politics, Aristotle's, 94
Pollio Eclogue, Virgil's, 198
Pollock, Sir Frederick, 137
Pollok, Robert, 101

Polycleitus, 79
Pope, Alexander, 21, 73, 74, 79, 134, 193
Pound, Ezra, 37
Ptolemy, 7
Puttenham, 39

Quarterly Review, 163, 164, 169

Racine, 13
Raleigh, Sir Walter, 96
Rameses, 7
Reade, Charles, 213
Renan, E., 27
Renouf, 53
Richards, Ivor Armstrong, 72, 75
Ridgeway, Sir William, 6
Ross, Martin (Violet Florence Martin), 196, 218 *et seq.*
Rousseau, 32, 33
Ruskin, John, 79, 199

Sappho, 9, 10
Schelling, 79
Schopenhauer, 79
Scott, Sir Walter, 63, 115, 116, 165, 167, 202, 213
Seward, Thomas, 2
Shakespeare, John, 159
Shakespeare, William, 29, 59, 63, 74, 76, 92, 112, 113, 118, 125, 130, 131, 132, 137 *et seq.*
Shelley, Percy Bysshe, 13, 14, 15, 37, 43, 63, 125, 166, 167, 168
Shirley, James, 27
Sidney, Algernon, 70
Sidney, Sir Philip, 39, 79, 161
Smith, Albert, 203
Socrates, 2, 45
Somerville, Edith Œnone, 196, 218 *et seq.*
Song of the Indian Maid, Keats', 84
Sonnets, Shakespeare's, 158
Southey, Robert, 166
Spanish Tragedy, The, 146
Spectator, The, 59, 67, 195
Spedding, James, 161
Spenser, Edmund, 63, 203
Spingarn, Professor J. E., 77, 78
Stevenson, Robert Louis, 127

INDEX

Strabo, 39
Strachey, Lytton, 31, 33

Taming of the Shrew, 146
Taylor, Jeremy, 48, 70
Tempest, The, 121, 125, 130, 152
Tennyson, Alfred, Lord, 29, 161 *et seq.*, 179, 185, 199
Terpander, 9
Tertullian, 4
Thackeray, William Makepeace, 36, 178, 203
Themistocles, 8
Theocritus, 185, 186
Thomas, Edward, 199, 200
Thompson, Francis, 66
Thompson, W. H., 161
Thothmes, 7
Thrasymachus, 45
Thucydides, 32, 57
Titus Andronicus, 147
Tolstoy, 213
Trench, Richard Chenevix, 161
Troilus and Cressida, 147, 149

Trollope, Anthony, 203
Tyrtaeus, 17

Vaughan, Henry, 27
Venice Preserved, 2
Venus and Adonis, 131
Vere, Aubrey, 167
Villon, 1
Vinci, Leonardo da, 13
Virgil, 112
Voltaire, 32, 33

Waller, Edmund, 127
Walton, Isaak, 106
Warren, Samuel, 203
Webbe, William, 39
White, Gilbert, 199, 200
Wilson, John (Christopher North), 165
Wood, Mrs Henry, 211
Wordsworth, William, 5, 13, 14, 37, 41, 65, 68, 69, 70, 75, 163, 166, 168, 171
Wykeham, William of, 49

CAMBRIDGE: PRINTED BY WALTER LEWIS, M.A., AT THE UNIVERSITY PRESS